Southern LIGHTHOUSES

OUTER BANKS *to* CAPE FLORIDA

Third Edition

PHOTOGRAPHS BY BRUCE ROBERTS
TEXT BY RAY JONES

The Globe Pequot Press

Guilford, Connecticut

Bodie Island Lighthouse

All photographs, unless otherwise credited, are by Bruce Roberts.
Book design by Nancy Freeborn
Map by Lisa Reneson

Library of Congress Cataloging-in-Publication Data
Roberts, Bruce, date
    Southern lighthouses: Outer Banks to Cape Florida/ photographs by Bruce Roberts; text by Ray Jones.—3rd ed.
        p. cm. — (Lighthouses series)
    Includes index.
    ISBN 0-7627-1243-0
        1. Lighthouses—South Atlantic States. I. Jones, Ray 1948– II. Title. III. Lighthouse series (Guilford, Conn.)

VK1024.S52 R63 2001
387.1'55'0975—dc21   2001053209

Front-cover photograph: Ponce de Leon Inlet Ligththouse, Florida
Back-cover photograph: Cape Hatteras Lighthouse, North Carolina

Printed in Quebec, Canada
Third Edition/First Printing

A summer view of Georgia's St. Simons Island Lighthouse.

Southern Lights

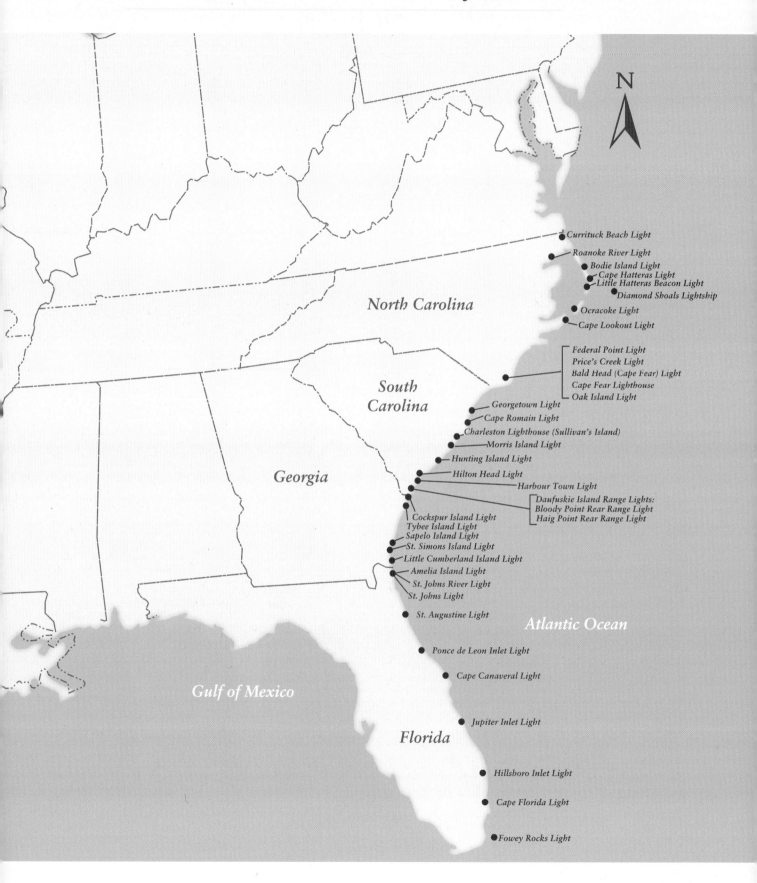

N

Currituck Beach Light
Roanoke River Light
Bodie Island Light
Cape Hatteras Light
Little Hatteras Beacon Light
Diamond Shoals Lightship
Ocracoke Light
Cape Lookout Light

North Carolina

Federal Point Light
Price's Creek Light
Bald Head (Cape Fear) Light
Cape Fear Lighthouse
Oak Island Light

South Carolina

Georgetown Light
Cape Romain Light
Charleston Lighthouse (Sullivan's Island)
Morris Island Light
Hunting Island Light
Hilton Head Light
Harbour Town Light

Daufuskie Island Range Lights:
Bloody Point Rear Range Light
Haig Point Rear Range Light

Georgia

Cockspur Island Light
Tybee Island Light
Sapelo Island Light
St. Simons Island Light
Little Cumberland Island Light
Amelia Island Light
St. Johns River Light
St. Johns Light

St. Augustine Light

Atlantic Ocean

Ponce de Leon Inlet Light

Cape Canaveral Light

Gulf of Mexico

Jupiter Inlet Light

Florida

Hillsboro Inlet Light

Cape Florida Light

Fowey Rocks Light

CONTENTS

ACKNOWLEDGMENTS

 our decades ago when I first started photographing lighthouses on the Outer Banks of North Carolina, it was not easy to reach some lighthouses, never mind capture them on film. I want to thank David Stick for driving me down the beach in his Jeep to the Cape Hatteras Lighthouse. That day we passed several shipwrecks before reaching the light station, and it was this trip that etched forever in my mind the images of lighthouses, dunes, time sealed in foundered ships, and the many treasures offered up by the sea following a storm.

There are many other individuals who have helped with the three editions and numerous printings of *Southern Lighthouses*. Thanks go to Aycock Brown. He was the one-man Dare County Tourist Bureau in the 1960s who generously shared his wealth of knowledge on lighthouses, shipwrecks, and fishing.

Appreciation also goes to Bob Woody of the Cape Hatteras National Seashore, who supervised the media during the relocation of the Cape Hatteras Lighthouse, and was always willing to help me take the photos needed for this book. I also thank Park Ranger Rob Bolling and Park Historian Steve Harrison. Big thanks go to Cape Lookout volunteer Richard Meissner who invited me to stay in the double keepers quarters on Core Banks Island. I enjoyed a memorable night with meteors streaking overhead, ocean sounds, and the sweep of the Cape Lookout beacon with a backdrop of a storm at sea. Captain Sandy of Captain Sandy's Tours took me out to the Georgetown Lighthouse in his boat and related myths and lore in a southern drawl I'll never forget. Thanks also to Steve Messengill of the North Carolina Department of Archives and History and Dr. Robert Browning at the U.S. Coast Guard Headquarters in Washington, D.C.

I want to recognize the Outer Banks History Center in Manteo, North Carolina, and its former director, Wynne Dough, and assistants Sarah Downing and Brian Edwards, for helping me with research and archival photographs.

And finally, I thank my wife, Cheryl, for putting up with long drives and late hours; for keeping notes that I would have otherwise lost; for carrying camera equipment up and down countless steps to lighthouses; and for her smile at the end of each exhausting day.

—*Bruce Roberts*

The Ponce Inlet Light against a fiery early evening sky.

A powerful Fresnel lens glows in its birdcage lantern room atop the Currituck Beach Lighthouse in Corolla, North Carolina. The lens throws out a focused beam that can be seen from 19 miles at sea. Fresnels came in a hierarchy of sizes, referred to as first-order, second-order, third-order, and so on. Among the standard Fresnels, the first-order lenses were the largest, with an inside diameter of roughly six feet. Only the most important coastal lights were given these expensive lenses.

INTRODUCTION

The epic poems of Homer, the blind bard of ancient Greece, celebrated many maritime wonders. Among these were the Sirens, mermaids whose seductive songs lured whole shiploads of sailors to destruction on jagged, wave-swept rocks; the Cyclopes, a race of one-eyed giants who sank ships by hurling boulders into the sea; a vast whirlpool capable of swallowing up entire fleets; a leather bag able to contain all of Earth's unfavorable winds; and that somewhat less mythical marvel still known and appreciated to this day—a lighthouse. The following passage from Homer's *Odyssey* contains what may be history's first literary mention of a navigational light:

> *Tonight wandering sailors pale with fears,*
> *Wide over the watery waste a light appears,*
> *On the far-seen mountain blazing high,*
> *Streams from lonely watchtower to the sky.*

Lighthouse history reaches back, not just to Homer's day (about 800 B.C.), but to the very dawn of civilization. No doubt the earliest maritime peoples banked fires on hills and mountainsides to call their sailors home from the sea. Later, ancient port cities in Sumer, Egypt, and Greece guided mariners into their bustling harbors with lights that shone from atop battlements or towers.

Two of the seven extraordinary man-made structures known collectively as the Wonders of the (Ancient) World were lighthouses. Built about 200 B.C., the famed Colossus of Rhodes marked a key island harbor frequented by Greek warships and trading vessels. A bronze statue of the god Helios, the Colossus stood more than 120 feet tall and held aloft a light that could be seen and followed by distant ships. Interestingly, the Statue of Liberty in New York was patterned after the Colossus, and she, too, once served as a harbor lighthouse.

Also listed among the Seven Wonders was Pharos, a 450-foot stone tower dominating the Greco-Egyptian city of Alexandria. At the top of the tower was a huge cauldron where bright fires were kept blazing all night. The orange glow of the flames could be seen from up to 30 miles out in the dark Mediterranean, and it guided a constant parade of Greek and Roman ships into the harbor. Once in Alexandria, the ships' bellies were filled to overflowing with the grain that grew in fabulous abundance in the nearby Nile Delta. Then the heavily laden grain ships fanned out across the sea to feed hungry peoples throughout the known world. Without this Egyptian grain—and the single great lighthouse that helped provide access to it—the Roman Empire might never have existed. Not only was Pharos the first great lighthouse known to history, it was also the tallest light and the one with the longest service record. Completed in 270 B.C., Pharos served Alexandria and Mediterranean mariners for more than 1,200 years before collapsing in an earthquake during the Middle Ages.

The lighthouses that brighten America's southern coast today are similar to the ancient Pharos in a number of ways. Like Pharos, which outlived both the Hellenic and the Roman civilizations, many of the South's lighthouses are, by American standards at least, quite old. Some have stood for almost two centuries. Like Pharos, they were originally built to serve a largely agrarian society. During the nineteenth century and for much of the twentieth century as well, the ships these lights guided into Charleston, Savannah, Wilmington, and other key southern ports came to load up on the cotton, tobacco, and sugar produced by southern farms and plantations. And while Pharos was history's tallest lighthouse, many of the towers that soar above the flat, sandy shores of the southern United States are among the tallest in America. The Cape Hatteras tower in North Carolina tops out at 192 feet, the Sullivans Island tower in South Carolina at 163 feet, the Tybee Island tower in Georgia at 144 feet, and the St. Augustine tower in Florida at 161 feet. These lofty lighthouse towers need their extraordinary height because of the unique geology of the American South.

MAN-MADE MOUNTAINS OF BRICK AND STONE

The southern Appalachians are like crotchety old men. Stooped, rounded, and gentle in appearance, they look harmless enough but have sharp tempers—as any climber caught in a thunderstorm on the side of one of these mountains will quickly learn. Although some of their domes are bald and, over the eons, gravity has pulled them ever closer to the plains below, they are still quite tall, some of them topping out at more than 6,000 feet. But they were once much taller.

When the Appalachians were young—more than one hundred million years ago—they reached several miles into the sky, and their height and grandeur would have rivaled that of today's Himalayas. At that time the ocean rolled in close to the foothills of the great mountains. There were no human mariners around to sail the waters off the primordial Appalachian coast, but had there been, they might have looked to the gleaming, snowcapped

Unlike the sea grass clinging stubbornly to this Outer Banks dune, the Cape Hatteras Light tower could not bend with the wind and the tide. In 1999 the historic brick edifice was moved more than a quarter mile inland to save it from encroaching ocean waves.

peaks for guidance. Nowadays, however, even the tallest of the Appalachians are much too far from the ocean to be of any use for navigation.

Although in most places it is buried under hundreds of feet of rock, geologists can trace the original Appalachian coast. Known today as the Fall-line, it forms a gradually curving arch linking the cities of Raleigh, North Carolina, Columbia, South Carolina, and Macon, Georgia, all of which are 150 miles or more from the Atlantic. Deep wells drilled along the Fall-line sometimes yield shark's teeth and the fossilized remains of extinct ocean species. Near Macon the decayed bones of shark and fish form thick deposits of a substance called kaolin, an ultra-white clay applied as a coating to high-quality printing paper like that used to make this book. But no sea creatures live close to the Fall-line today. Over millions of years the steadily eroding mountains have filled offshore areas with rock and sand, pushing the ocean and the shore far to the east. The Outer Banks and the South's other barrier islands, which have risen from the sea only since the end of the last ice age—about 10,000 years ago—show that this land-building process continues even today. This unending struggle between mountains and gravity, the stubborn ocean and the emerging land, has produced the southern landscape as we know it today.

Among America's foremost—and most frequently overlooked—natural treasures is the long, graceful coastline of the South. Washed by some of the nation's cleanest salt waters, more than 1,100 miles of blazing white beaches stretch between the North Carolina Outer Banks and the southern tip of Florida. Behind the beaches, sand piles up into great dunes and barrier islands protecting ancient groves of hardwood, vast lakes of tall marsh grass, and extensive estuaries rich in shrimp and crab. And on the mainland, just beyond the reach of the ocean, is the southern "low country," which blesses farmers with soil so rich that, in earlier times, it could make a plantation owner rich with a single year's plantings.

Standing guard over all this natural wealth are the stone, brick, concrete, and metal sentinels that are the subject of this book. Without their tall towers to serve as daymarks and their bright beacons to provide guidance at night, navigating this economically vital stretch of coastline would be much more difficult and dangerous. While these flat, almost featureless shores appear harmless, to mariners they are as threatening as any on the planet. Here ship-

A burst of sunlight reflected by a lantern-room window gives the St. Simons Light-house some extra flash. (Courtesy Mark Riddick, New Light Photography)

killing shoals, shallows, and hurricanes play the roles of Sirens and one-eyed giants, and they are just as deadly. So many ships and sailors have met their end in the shallows and pounding surf off these shores that the area is known as the Graveyard of the Atlantic.

Nowadays, satellites, radar, and other sophisticated technology make it possible for navigators to pinpoint their positions at any time of the day or night. Even so, sailors still anxiously scan the horizon in search of lights, buoys, and familiar points of land. They find the sight of a lighthouse beacon comforting, particularly along the southern coast, where there are so many threats and so few natural seamarks.

Today lighthouses and lesser navigational markers form an unbroken chain of lights from Maine to Florida. But this was not always the case. Before the nineteenth century brought a flurry of lighthouse construction, the southern coastline, especially, remained a dark and foreboding landfall. Countless sailors and hapless passengers paid with their lives for the absence of lights to guide their vessels. The following passage relates the tragic story of the *Tyrrel,* lost off Cape Hatteras in 1759. The *Tyrrel* was only one of the thousands of ships that suffered a similar fate. Most of *their* stories will never be known.

WITH NO LIGHT TO GUIDE THEM

On the last Saturday in June, in the year 1759, a handsome merchant brig known as the *Tyrrel* set sail from New York bound for Antigua in the West Indies. Capt. Arthur Cochlan kept the *Tyrrel* close-in, just beyond sight of the land, so that he could take advantage of the coast-hugging Labrador Current. Cochlan's brig made good progress, and by the evening of July 1, it approached Cape Hatteras.

Cochlan planned to keep well to seaward, rounding the cape to avoid Diamond Shoals, the deadly finger of sand that protrudes some 8 miles from Hatteras out into the Atlantic. But in the end the shoals would not be his chief concern, for just after dark, the *Tyrrel* slammed head-on into a squall.

Hearing the wind claw at the *Tyrrel*'s two big masts, Cochlan ordered his crew to close-reef the topsails. But the wind grew stronger, the waves surged higher, and soon the *Tyrrel* began to take on water. Cochlan decided to make a run through Hatteras Inlet toward the calmer waters of Pamlico Sound. The *Tyrrel* never made it to the inlet. Just as the ship turned toward land, it was hit by an enormously powerful gust of wind. The *Tyrrel* rolled over on its side and started to sink.

Some members of the crew were belowdecks when the *Tyrrel* capsized. The impact of the gust threw First Mate Thomas Purnell out of his bunk and against the wall of his cabin. Purnell fought his way to the roundhouse door, where he barely managed to avoid being crushed by a huge ladder that had broken away from the quarterdeck. Soon he was in the water, swimming for his life along with most of his shipmates.

Some of the crew remained with the brig and tried to right it by shifting the weight of its two heavy guns. But Purnell saw that the only hope lay in the lifeboat now floating bottom-side up some distance from the hulk of the doomed *Tyrrel.* Purnell and several other sailors swam out to the boat and managed to turn it over.

Filled with water to within 3 or 4 inches of its gunwales, the boat was useless. But the cabin boy, being the lightest member of the crew, slipped on board and set to work with a bucket. In about half an hour he had the boat more or less dry, and half-drowned sailors started to clamber aboard. Eventually, seventeen men were crammed into the boat, which was only 19 feet long.

Tragically, the carpenter had lost all his tools in the wreck. With a decent chisel he might have been able to cut through the sides of the capsized ship and get at its ample stores. As it was, not a single barrel of fresh water and only one small chest of biscuit could be located among the flotsam littering the water near the sinking brig.

The darkness surrounding the men in the boat was total. Captain Cochlan believed he was very near Cape Hatteras, but in 1759, no lighthouse stood on the cape. If there had been a light burning on the cape that evening, the crew of the *Tyrrel* might not have suffered the awful fate that awaited them. But with his compass ruined by seawater and no stars in the sky, the captain had no way to take bearings. He looked in every direction and saw no lights at all on any horizon. So, with a deep sigh, he pointed, and his men began to pull toward what they desperately hoped was dry land and safety.

At dawn on the following day, Cochlan could see that he had pointed in the wrong direction. There was no land in sight. He had taken his boat toward the east, away from Hatteras. Cochlan's crew turned their little vessel back toward land, but later that day, they encountered a westerly wind that made progress impossible. In fact, the winds blew up into a storm that carried them farther and farther out onto the high sea.

On the third day the men gave up most of their clothing so that the cloth could be stitched into a makeshift sail. Using an oar as mast, they raised their sail, and the sluggish forward motion it gave their boat filled them with hope. Guiding on the sun during the day and the North Star at night, Cochlan maintained a dead-reckoning course for Cape Hatteras. But still he could not find land.

On July 11, after more than nine days in the open boat, Cochlan's men began to die. Some, maddened by thirst, had started to drink seawater. The second mate, who had begun to drink great, heaping handfuls of the killing salt water, was the first to go. An hour or so later, he was followed by the carpenter, who had also taken to drinking seawater. The bodies, by necessity, were dumped overboard.

At dawn on July 12, a sloop was sighted on the horizon, causing an eruption of shouting and waving on board the *Tyrrel*

Like a giant barber pole, the St. Augustine Lighthouse towers above the lighthouse's entryway. Note the date over the door.

launch. But the sloop vanished as quickly as it had appeared, and the now hopelessly weakened sailors gave themselves up for lost. By the next morning, three more men had died. Another perished later that same day. Four died on July 14 and three on July 15.

That left only Captain Cochlan, First Mate Purnell, the boatswain, and the cabin boy. Purnell believed the cabin boy would be the last left alive, but on the evening of July 15, the lad breathed his last. The three survivors then made an agonizing decision; they would cut pieces of flesh off the boy's dead body and eat them. In the end, however, they were too squeamish to carry out the plan.

Some days later Purnell found himself alone in the boat. For nearly a week he drifted in a thick fog, keeping himself alive by scraping barnacles off the sides and rudder of the boat with a knife and chewing them. Then, on July 24, the fog cleared, and on the horizon, Purnell spotted a sail. There was a ship—a sloop headed in his direction.

After more than three weeks in an open boat with no fresh water and only barnacles for food, Purnell was pulled aboard a merchant vessel about two days out from Marblehead, Massachusetts. The *Tyrrel* launch had drifted into the Gulf Stream and been pushed far to the north. The captain of the rescuing ship, a man named Castleman, carried the wretched castaway down to his own cabin and fed him some thin soup. A few days later Purnell's shriveled feet touched land again at Marblehead.

It took Purnell two months to recover from his ordeal, and by then the American colonies were abuzz over his miraculous survival and rescue. The tragic fate of the *Tyrrel,* with the loss of all but one member of its crew, brought heated demands that a lighthouse be erected on Cape Hatteras. But more than forty years and a revolution would pass before a lighthouse was finally built on the cape to guide mariners and warn them away from Hatteras's treacherous shoals.

The lamps of the Cape Hatteras Light were first lit during the summer of 1803. By that time, only a few other lighthouses stood on the sandy coasts

The recently restored and repainted Tybee Island Lighthouse near Savannah, Georgia.

and barrier islands of the states south of the Chesapeake, the most notable of them at Cape Fear in North Carolina, Charleston Harbor in South Carolina, and Tybee Island near Savannah, Georgia.

But the Lighthouse Service, formed by act of Congress in 1789, was well aware of the dangers the southern coastline represented to mariners. Obviously, the few lights then in existence were woefully inadequate. Southbound ships had to hug those coasts to avoid fighting the strong northward current of the Gulf Stream. This made them vulnerable to shoals and to being driven ashore by storms. To lessen the dangers, the service (later known as the Lighthouse Board) embarked on a construction program that, after many decades, would dot the southern coasts with tall lighthouses.

Like the ill-fated Tyrrel, *countless vessels have ended their seafaring days on the sands of the Outer Banks. These fractured ribs are all that remain of the* Laura E. Barnes.

CHAPTER ONE

NORTH CAROLINA:

Lights of the Big Sand Islands

O ut in the Atlantic off the coast of North Carolina, the ocean is constantly at war with itself. Here the steamy Gulf Stream swirls up from the Caribbean to meet the cold Labrador Current, which has pushed down a thousand miles or more from the Arctic. These two rivers of seawater, each of them mightier than the Mississippi, slam into each other with a violence that can churn up hurricane-force winds, swallow up whole ships, and reshape entire coastlines.

Long ago these titanic forces helped build the Outer Banks, that long, narrow string of sandy islands rising unexpectedly from the ocean 70 miles or so from the mainland. The powerful currents that built the islands also tend to push ships much too close to them, with the result that the banks have become a sort of maritime graveyard. At least 2,300 major vessels have come to grief here, along with many thousands more of their hapless passengers and crews. One such victim was the brig *Tyrrel* (its destruction is described in the previous section), swept away with all but a single member of its crew in 1759. Another was the Civil War ironclad *Monitor,* which had only recently survived its point-blank cannon-to-cannon face-off with the Confederate warship *Virginia.*

SAVING AN AMERICAN LEGEND

Since 1803 one of the nation's most famous and important man-made structures has fought back against the ship-killing Atlantic by warning mariners to keep away from the Outer Banks. Perhaps the world's best-known traffic light, its signal is observed and obeyed by ships' captains and navigators every night of the year. Soaring more than 190 feet above the island sands, its black-and-white, barber pole–striped tower is almost as well known and beloved as the Statue of Liberty, the Empire State Building, or the Golden Gate Bridge.

Until recently, this widely recognized national treasure was threatened by the very same natural forces that make the North Carolina coast such a dangerous place for ships. Since the end of the last ice age about 10,000 years ago, the Atlantic has shaped and reshaped the Outer Banks while pushing the islands slowly but steadily westward. When the existing Cape Hatteras Lighthouse was completed in 1870, replacing an early tower dating to 1803, it stood at least 1,600 feet from the ocean. Within little more than a century, however, the Atlantic had cut away so much of the island that the Atlantic's destructive tides had rolled to within a mere hundred feet of the tower's foundation.

Over the years many attempts were made to halt the ocean's advance. Government engineers

The Cape Hatteras Lighthouse as it looked while under assault by the Atlantic during the 1990s. The massive tower was moved to a safer location in 1999.

Excavating the old foundation beneath the Cape Hatteras tower and preparing the 3,500-ton structure for relocation. The keeper's house on the move (middle right). The opposite page depicts the carefully graded move corridor with insets showing the tower on its original site and Hatteras designer Dexter Stetson.

The Cape Hatteras Lighthouse was moved just in time. Only a few days after the relocation was completed, a powerful hurricane struck the area. The inset above shows tower glass shattered by the storm.

built massive stone and concrete groins or walls to trap sand as it migrated along the shore, pumped in additional sand to replenish eroded sections of beach, and even planted artificial seaweed to stabilize the sands just offshore. But nothing worked for long. By the 1990s, the waves were coming so close that some observers predicted the historic tower would fall during the next big storm. It had become apparent that the only way to save the lighthouse was to move it.

The idea of relocating a 192-foot tall, 3,500-ton brick tower may have seemed fantastic, but boosted by a $12 million federal appropriation, the project was undertaken during the late spring of 1999. The International Chimney Company of Buffalo, New York, was selected to do the engineering and oversee the actual move. The company had already successfully relocated Rhode Island's historic Southeast Lighthouse on Block Island. The earlier move, completed in 1993, was accomplished without the loss of a single brick from the 120-year-old, Victorian-style structure.

The technique for moving the Cape Hatteras Lighthouse was similar to the one used on Block Island. First the ground around the base of the structure was excavated and the stone foundation removed and replaced by steel supports. Poised on a platform of heavy steel beams, the tower was then pushed on specially designed rollers along a series of rails by powerful hydraulic jacks. Moving at a speed so slow that its motion was barely perceptible, the tower inched along its rails, which were lubricated with ordinary household soap. It took more than three weeks to move the mighty structure to its new home, 2,900 feet from its original position and more than 1,600 feet inland from the Atlantic tides.

The dramatic move of the Cape Hatteras Lighthouse attracted television camera crews, photographers, and journalists from all over the world. Networks and news agencies issued daily reports on the tower's progress as it moved along at an average speed of approximately 125 feet a day. Begun at 3:05 P.M. on June 17, 1999, the relocation was completed shortly after 1:20 P.M. on July 9, 1999.

Now resting on a new and stronger foundation, the old tower is likely to survive for at least another century. A matchless symbol of our nation's maritime past has been preserved. Both a victory for historic preservation and a monumental engineering achievement, the move of the Cape Hatteras Lighthouse will be remembered for generations to come.

CURRITUCK BEACH LIGHT

Corolla, North Carolina – 1875

Near the border between North Carolina and Virginia, the mighty Gulf Stream sweeps in close to the mainland. To avoid fighting its powerful northeasterly current, the captains of southbound ships must steer perilously close to land. Sometimes they come too close, with disastrous results, for these are dangerous waters where even a small navigational error can be fatal. Here, ship-killing shoals and shallows reach far out into the sea, and over the years they have claimed countless vessels along with their passengers and crews.

For hundreds of years—the first Spanish ships sailed along this coast in the early 1500s—seamen could count on little or no guidance from the shore. The low, nearly featureless sandy islands offered few clues for a navigator struggling to determine his ship's position. Often the beaches and the tangled forests behind them could not even be seen—that is, until it was too late.

Then, late in 1875, mariners could see a powerful light shining from a high brick tower at Currituck Beach near the seaside town of Corolla, North Carolina. Its lamps first lit in December of that year, the Currituck Beach Lighthouse illuminated one of the last remaining dark stretches of southern coastline. Strategically placed about halfway between the Cape Henry, Virginia, and Bodie Island lights, the Currituck Lighthouse filled a menacing gap in the chain of navigational lights stretching along the U.S. coast from Maine to Florida.

The 162-foot Currituck Beach tower was the last in a series of three key coastal sentinels built in North Carolina during a five-year span from 1870 to 1875. The first was the present 193-foot Cape Hatteras tower, completed in 1870. From Hatteras, construction crews moved on to Bodie Island, where they had a 163-foot lighthouse tower standing and in operation by 1872.

At Currituck Beach, however, the work would not go so smoothly. The shifting sands underlying the construction site presented builders with special difficulties. How could they provide the giant tower with a stable foundation? To solve this problem, they hammered pilings deep into the sand, overlaying them with a framework of timbers and a stone bed almost 7 feet thick.

To help the lighthouse withstand the high winds of storms that often blow in off the Atlantic, they gave it stout brick walls almost 6 feet thick at the base, tapering to 3 feet thick at the top. In all, the work took almost three years and was not completed until late in 1875. The time and effort were well spent, however, since the Currituck Beach tower has successfully weathered more than a century's worth of gales and hurricanes.

So that mariners could distinguish the tower from others to the north and south, its red bricks were left unpainted, and they remain so today. The 12-foot-tall lantern at the top of the tower still holds the original

The handsomely restored Currituck Beach keeper's residence as viewed through a window near the top of the tower.

first-order Fresnel lens in nightly use now for more than 125 years. The massive French-made bull's-eye lens focuses the station's light into powerful white flashes that can be spotted from up to 19 miles away. One flash is seen approximately every twenty seconds.

During the nineteenth century the light was provided by lard oil lamps and the lens rotated by means of a giant clockwork mechanism driven by huge weights descending through the center of the tower. Several times every night the keepers had to climb the tower's 214 steps to fuel the lamps or crank the weights back to the top. Nowadays, of course, the lamps are electrified and the mechanism is motor driven. The keepers, who once lived with their families in a spacious duplex beside the tower, have been absent since 1939, when the Coast Guard automated the station.

For years the keeper's dwelling and other buildings at the Currituck Beach station were sadly neglected and allowed to fall into ruin. In 1981, however, the property was leased to the Outer Banks Conservationists of nearby Manteo, North Carolina, and this preservation-minded group has restored the old lighthouse to its former glory. The ornate keeper's duplex has been handsomely refurbished and an adjacent building restored to serve as a museum and gift shop. The Currituck Beach Lighthouse is listed on the National Register of Historic Places.

HOW TO GET THERE: *From Kitty Hawk turn north off US 158 (the Outer Banks Highway) onto State 12 and drive approximately 20 miles to the village of Corolla. The lighthouse is on the left and can be seen from the road. The Outer Banks Conservationists operate the station visitors center and gift shop. Those who wish to climb the tower's 214 steps must pay a small fee, but the extraordinary view from the gallery is well worth the price. The station is open to the public every day except Sunday during warm-weather months. For information write to Currituck Beach Lighthouse, P.O. Box 58, Corolla, NC 27929 or call (252) 453–8152.*

The Corolla/Currituck Beach area may also be a good place to catch a glimpse of one of the Outer Banks's last herds of wild horses. Information on the horses is available from the lighthouse or the Corolla Wild Horse Fund at the aforementioned address and phone number. The Fund solicits donations and offers memberships to those who would like to help preserve the wild herds.

This spiral staircase leads to the top of the 162-foot tower. Keepers climbed its 214 steps several times each night.

BODIE ISLAND LIGHT

Bodie Island, North Carolina — 1847, 1859, AND 1872

In 1837 Congress sent Lieut. Napoleon Coste, commander of the revenue cutter *Campbell*, to inspect the dark coasts south of the Chesapeake. After rounding Cape Henry and losing sight of its sandstone lighthouse tower, Coste found no other worthwhile navigational markers until he reached Cape Hatteras, more than 150 miles to the south. Coste reported that a lighthouse was urgently needed to fill in this huge blind spot. He recommended that the new lighthouse be located on Bodie Island, at the northern end of the Outer Banks, where "more vessels are lost . . . than on any other part of our coast."

With Coste's report in hand, Congress appropriated $5,000 to build a lighthouse, not on Bodie, but on adjacent Pea Island. When Bodie was finally chosen as the new site, problems with purchasing the land and squabbles over the location and design of the tower caused a ten-year delay in construction, which did not begin until the summer of 1847.

The contractor on the project was Francis Gibbons of Baltimore, who would later become prominent as a builder of lighthouses on the rugged West Coast. Unfortunately, the highly competent Gibbons was not allowed to design the tower. Instead, he was handed a plan for a squat, ungainly structure only 54 feet high and measuring 17 feet in diameter at the base and 12½ feet in diameter at the top.

Gibbons was forced to work under the thumb of an ex-customs inspector who knew little about construction and even less about lighthouse towers. Although Gibbons and his men struck mud only a few feet below the Bodie Island sands, the contractor was told to drive no piles. Instead, he was instructed to lay down a shallow foundation of brick. As a result, the tower was highly unstable, and soon after it was completed in 1848, it began to lean sickeningly toward the sea.

Within two years of construction, the tower was already a foot out of plumb and leaning farther to the

Insulated from winter chill by the broad North Carolina sounds, Bodie Island rarely sees snow, but the late December day depicted here was an exception.

As evening approaches the sun bids farewell to the Bodie Island Lighthouse. Soon the powerful Bodie beacon will light up the sky.

Confederate troops stacked explosives inside the tower and blew it apart.

A third Bodie Island Lighthouse was completed in 1872. It was designed and built by Dexter Stetson, who also built the Cape Hatteras Lighthouse. Materials left over from the construction of the Cape Hatteras Tower were used to build structures for the off-loading of equipment and supplies onto Bodie Island. Rising 156 feet above sea level, the Bodie tower held a first-order Fresnel lens, its light visible from 19 miles at sea. Within a month of the lighting, geese crashed into the lantern, badly damaging the lens, but it was repaired and is still in use. The tower is painted with white and black horizontal bands for better visibility as a daymark.

Although automated in 1931, when its beacon was electrified, the Bodie Island Lighthouse remains vital to navigation. The lantern retains its original giant lens, which produces white flashes every thirty seconds. The powerful beacon can be seen from a distance of approximately 19 miles.

HOW TO GET THERE: *One of the most scenic light stations in the eastern United States, the Bodie Island Lighthouse is open daily to the public. It is located on State 12, about 17 miles north of Rodanthe and a few miles south of the Cape Hatteras National Seashore entrance. A sign points the way to the lighthouse, which can be reached via a paved road off State 12. The keeper's dwelling, built in 1893, now serves as the lighthouse visitors center. Operated by the National Park Service, it contains a small museum highlighting the history of the Bodie Island Station and of other lighthouses on the Outer Banks. For information contact the Cape Hatteras National Seashore, Route 1, Box 675, Manteo, NC 27954; (252) 473–2111.*

Visitors to the Bodie Island Lighthouse will want to stop at Rodanthe for a look at the Chicamacomico Lifesaving Station. Built in 1911, the station has been handsomely restored and contains a pair of fascinating museums dedicated to the old U.S. Lifesaving Service. The station and museums are open May through September from 11:00 A.M. to 5:00 P.M. on Tuesday, Thursday, and Saturday. For information write to Chicamacomico Historical Association, Inc., Box 5, Rodanthe, NC 27968.

east with each passing day. To keep the lighthouse from toppling over, the government spent $1,400 trying to straighten it. But the tower continued to wobble on its unsteady base, leaning first one way and then another.

By 1859 the Bodie Island Lighthouse had deteriorated beyond the possibility of repair, and the Lighthouse Board secured a $25,000 appropriation from Congress to erect a new tower. Built on sturdy piles, the new lighthouse was 80 feet tall. Its lantern held a third-order Fresnel lens, but its lamps, first lit on July 1, 1859, would burn for little more than two years. In the fall of 1861,

Squeezed between the Atlantic and North Carolina sounds, Bodie Island confounded early lighthouse builders with its damp, sandy soil. The island's first tower settled rapidly, developed a pronounced lean, and had to be abandoned. Built on a granite foundation, the existing tower has stood straight since 1872.

CAPE HATTERAS LIGHT

Hatteras Island, North Carolina — 1803, 1870

America's Mercury and Apollo astronauts were told to watch for the hook of Cape Hatteras when their orbits carried them over the East Coast of the United States. Hatteras is such a prominent feature, it can easily be distinguished, even from hundreds of miles out in space. But earthly mariners have often had a difficult time seeing the cape, especially at night or in foul weather.

Two mighty rivers in the ocean, the cold Labrador Current flowing down from the north and the warm Gulf Stream sweeping up from the Caribbean, pass close by Cape Hatteras. Their strong currents push ships dangerously close to Hatteras and to Diamond

Shoals, the shallow bar extending 8 miles out into the ocean. As a result, this stormy coast, known to sailors as the Graveyard of the Atlantic, has claimed more than 2,300 ships since the early 1500s.

During colonial times, the British became all too well acquainted with the dangers of Cape Hatteras and her deadly shoals. The ill-fated *Tyrrel* was only one of countless colonial ships that ended their days in the shallows off the coast of North Carolina. But the British Parliament showed little interest in spending money on lighthouses in America, and nothing was done about placing a light on the cape until after the Revolutionary War.

Congress authorized construction of the Hatteras Lighthouse as early as 1794, but no brick was laid until late in 1799. The delay was caused, in part, by a political tiff over the selection of a contractor. The job eventually went to Henry Dearborn, a congressman who would later serve as secretary of war (the town of Dearborn, Michigan, is named after him). Dearborn's crews, tortured by swarms of mosquitoes and outbreaks of yellow fever, needed three years to complete the 95-foot tower. The light finally went into service in October 1803.

From the beginning the Hatteras Light had a spotty reputation as a coastal marker. Fitted with eighteen lamps and 14-inch reflectors, the light could supposedly be seen from 18 miles at sea. But ships' captains complained incessantly that they could not see the light, even when nearing the cape. In a report to the Lighthouse Board in 1851, U.S. Navy lieutenant David Porter called Hatteras "the worst light in the world."

Describing his many journeys around the cape, Porter said: "The first nine trips I made I never saw Hatteras Light at all, though frequently passing in sight of the breakers, and when I did see it, I could not tell it from a steamer's light, except that the steamers' lights are much brighter." In response to Porter's report and to the numerous complaints received about the

Now safe from the encroaching Atlantic, the Cape Hatteras Lighthouse proudly flies Old Glory. This Outer Banks light station has been an official U.S. government installation for two centuries.

Hatteras Light, the Lighthouse Board ordered the tower raised to 150 feet and had it fitted with a first-order Fresnel lens.

At the beginning of the Civil War, the Confederates removed the lens and destroyed the lighting apparatus. The Union had the lighthouse back in service again by June 1862, but mariners still considered it inadequate to its task. So, following the war, the board replaced it with a new, 193-foot brick tower, making Hatteras the tallest brick lighthouse in the United States.

The revolving first-order Fresnel lens atop the new tower was in operation by mid-December 1870. Shortly afterward, the old tower was blown up to keep it from falling over in a storm and damaging the new lighthouse or, perhaps, crushing some hapless assistant keeper. After the demolition the keeper reported sadly that the "old landmark was spread out on the beach, a mass of ruins."

The existing Cape Hatteras Lighthouse might have followed its predecessor into oblivion except for the extraordinary and expensive effort put forward to save it (see pages 9–12).

Originally, the lighthouse stood almost a quarter mile from the ocean, but storm-driven tides sweeping

Thrown up on the Outer Banks beaches by a storm, a World War II LST (Landing Ship Tank) fights its last battle with the Atlantic.

Cape Hatteras Light Station keepers and their families led a spartan life in 1901. Even at that time, the ocean threatened the existence of the lighthouse. Note the flooding in the foreground. (Courtesy U.S. Coast Guard)

For years government agencies had attempted to counter nature's assault on the Cape Hatteras Lighthouse by pumping fresh sand onto nearby beaches. They also tried using sandbags, steel groins, riprap, and even artificial seaweed, but nothing could hold back the Atlantic. In the end, moving the historic structure proved the only practical way to save it.

along the face of sandy Hatteras Island cut ever closer to the foundation of the massive tower. Eventually, the surf threatened to undermine its foundation. If nothing had been done to save the old tower, this historic national treasure would have toppled over onto the beach.

Fortunately for those who love lighthouses and for mariners who have depended on its guidance for almost 200 years, the Cape Hatteras Lighthouse still stands. Its light still shines each night, flashing white every seven and one half seconds from an elevation of 191 feet above high water. In clear weather it can be seen from a distance of almost 24 miles. Listed on the National Register of Historic Places, the old lighthouse remains a much-loved attraction of the Cape Hatteras National Seashore.

HOW TO GET THERE: *The Hatteras Light can be reached on paved road by taking US 64 at Manteo or US 158 down the Outer Banks past Kitty Hawk to the entrance of the National Seashore. State 12 runs more than 40 miles down the barrier dune islands. To reach the lighthouse, turn off State 12 at the village of Buxton. The tower is visible for miles.*

Pieces of the Civil War ironclad Monitor *and other bits of the Graveyard of the Atlantic are on display in a small maritime museum operated by the park service.*

For additional information contact the Cape Hatteras National Seashore, Route 1, Box 675, Manteo, NC 27954; (252) 473–2111.

To learn how you can join in the continuing effort to preserve the Cape Hatteras Lighthouse, contact the Outer Banks Lighthouse Society, P.O. Box 1005, Moorhead City, NC 28557; www.outerbanks.com/lighthouse-society.

LITTLE HATTERAS BEACON LIGHT
Cape Hatteras Island, North Carolina — 1856

Ironically, this diminutive lighthouse stood practically in the shadow of one of the nation's grandest light towers—Cape Hatteras. Only 25 feet tall—its neighbor soared more than 190 feet—the Little Hatteras Beacon Lighthouse was built in 1856 to guide vessels passing between the cape and the treacherous Diamond Shoals located several miles offshore. Bowled over by a hurricane in 1897, it was never replaced.

A submarine sand spit extends more than 8 miles into the Atlantic from the tip of Cape Hatteras. The lighthouse never adequately guarded the full length of the shoal. To protect ships from this dangerous obstacle, officials resorted to lightships, such as the one below, and later to the oil rig–style steel tower on the left, completed in 1967. The Hatteras Lightship had a unique history. It was sunk by a German submarine in World War I after attempting to alert U.S. warships of the enemy's presence. (Both photos courtesy U.S. Coast Guard)

OCRACOKE LIGHT

Ocracoke Island, North Carolina – 1803 AND 1823

During the early eighteenth century, the notorious pirate Edward Teach, also known as Blackbeard, ravaged the sea-lanes off the North Carolina Outer Banks. When not plundering helpless merchant ships, Blackbeard used Ocracoke Inlet as a convenient anchorage, and it was here, on November 21, 1718, that a pair of British sloops finally cornered the pirate.

Blackbeard had his opponents outgunned, and with the eight big cannons on his pirate ship, he shot the two small sloops to splinters. Even so, he could not prevent

The Ocracoke Light guards a former haunt of the famous pirate Blackbeard.

(Courtesy Mark Riddick, New Light Photography)

the stubborn British from boarding his vessel. Armed with pistols and rapiers, the British sailors swarmed over the gunwales behind their young commander, Lieut. Robert Maynard. At first the pirates had the upper hand, but they were soon exhausted from the effort of swinging their heavy cutlasses. The British, with their lightweight rapiers, moved in for the kill. Among the pirates cut down in the free-for-all was Blackbeard himself, who received numerous pistol wounds as well as a deep gash in his neck before falling dead on the blood-soaked deck of his ship.

(Photo courtesy Mark Riddick, New Light Photography)

The first Ocracoke Lighthouse was built in 1803 on Shell Castle Island inside the Ocracoke Inlet, not far from Blackbeard's former hideout. Destroyed by lightning on August 16, 1818, it was replaced some five years later by a light on the banks of the inlet near Ocracoke Village. This second light, built in 1823, remains among the oldest lighthouses still active on the southern coast.

In 1861 Confederate raiders destroyed the fourth-order Fresnel lens. A new lens was placed in the tower in 1864, and the Ocracoke Light has functioned continuously ever since. Located about a mile from the channel it guards, the Ocracoke Lighthouse is considered an inlet light rather than a coastal light.

Automated in 1955, the Ocracoke Lighthouse displays a fixed white light with a focal plane about 75 feet above high water. The light can be seen from approximately 14 miles away. Listed on the National Register of Historic Places, the station is managed by the National Park Service, which has restored the keeper's dwelling for use by National Seashore personnel.

HOW TO GET THERE: *Ocracoke Island can only be reached by ferry from Cedar Island, Swans Quarter, or Hatteras Island. Schedules vary according to the time of year. The ferries from Cedar Island and Swans Quarter take more than two hours and give travelers the feeling they are taking an ocean cruise. For departure times, fares, and other information, contact the North Carolina Department of Transportation, Ferry Division, 113 Arendell Street, Morehead City, NC 28557; (800) 293–3779. During the summer, especially, reservations are a must. The lighthouse is located off State 12 on Lighthouse Road a little more than a mile north of the main ferry landing or about 12 miles south of the Hatteras Inlet ferry landing. A small parking area allows visitors access to the station grounds and tower. Visitors are not allowed to climb the tower.*

For additional information contact the Cape Hatteras National Seashore at Route 1, Box 675, Manteo, NC 27954; (252) 473– 2111.

CAPE LOOKOUT LIGHT

Cape Lookout National Seashore, North Carolina – 1812 AND 1859

The harbor guarded by Cape Lookout has been a place of refuge for mariners sailing under the flags of many nations as well as under the skull and crossbones of piracy. Blackbeard is said to have dropped anchor in the harbor. It was used as an anchorage by the British during the Revolutionary War and by the U.S. Navy during two world wars. But the headland protecting this safe harbor from the open sea has always been considered extremely dangerous. Very early on, Cape Lookout earned the title *Promontorium Tremendum,* or "Horrible Headland," by smashing the hulls of ships that strayed too close to its hidden shoals.

Congress authorized a lighthouse for Cape Lookout in 1804, not long after the completion of the Hatteras Light. But as with the Hatteras Light and many other southern lighthouses, there were long delays in con-

struction of the tower, and it was not lighted until 1812. This first Cape Lookout Lighthouse cost $20,678 to build and was of unusual design. It consisted of an inner tower of brick enveloped by an outer cocoon of wood.

Painted with red and white stripes, the tower rose 104 feet above the water, but its light was surprisingly weak. Skippers often had a difficult time seeing it. David Porter, while a mail-steamer captain, complained that on more than one occasion he almost ran up on the shoals while looking for the light.

To improve the light's performance, the Lighthouse Board had a new, 156-foot tower constructed in 1859, fitting it with a first-order Fresnel lens. Confederates retreating from nearby Fort Macon knocked out the lens, but the board quickly replaced it with a third-order

For more than 190 years the Cape Lookout Light Station has guided mariners along the coast and warned them away from the dangerous shoals just offshore.

Fresnel, and the light remained in service. In 1873 the tower was painted with the unusual diamond pattern that still distinguishes it from other lights today.

Eventually the tower's lantern was refitted with a first-order Fresnel lens, which threw its powerful light out over the Atlantic each night for almost a century. In 1967, some years after the station was automated, the big Fresnel was removed and replaced by an airport-style beacon. After sitting in a crate for more than twenty-five years, the huge lens was installed in the recently relocated and refurbished Block Island Southeast Lighthouse in Rhode Island.

Despite the loss of its venerable lens, the Cape Lookout Lighthouse remains one of North Carolina's architectural treasures, and it is listed on the National Register of Historic Places. With its modern optic, it still does its nightly work of marking the cape and making coastal navigation safer. Flashing white every fifteen seconds from an elevation of 156 feet above high water, the light can be seen from up to 25 miles away under clear conditions.

Like the tower at Cape Hatteras, this historic lighthouse is threatened by beach erosion. When a 1933 hurricane opened up nearby Barden Channel, it may have doomed the tower. Over the decades since, the current has steadily gnawed away at the shoreline, and the water now stands only 250 feet from the tower's foundation. Unless something is done soon to stop the advance of the channel, it will eventually undercut and topple the old lighthouse.

HOW TO GET THERE: *The lighthouse is located on Core Banks Island, which is part of Cape Lookout National Seashore. The island can only be reached by passenger ferry. From Morehead City follow US 70 through Beaufort; at Otway turn toward Harkers Island and follow signs to the visitors center. Several privately operated passenger ferries in this area provide access to the lighthouse itself.*

The seashore headquarters is located on Harkers Island. For more information contact Cape Lookout National Seashore, 131 Charles Street, Harkers Island, NC 28531; (252) 728–2250.

While in the area, don't miss the North Carolina Maritime Museum in Beaufort. Among many other fascinating exhibits, it has on display a fourth-order Fresnel lens dating to 1892. For information contact the North Carolina Maritime Museum, 315 Front Street, Beaufort, NC 28516; (252) 728–7317.

PRICE'S CREEK LIGHTHOUSE
Southport, North Carolina

The ruins of the Price's Creek Lighthouse can be seen from the decks of the South-port–Fort Fisher Ferry (for ferry information see the Bald Head Light section). It was one of a series of range lights guiding vessels to the strategic port of Wilmington along a 26-mile stretch of the Cape Fear River. The other towers were destroyed by Confed-erate troops during the Civil War. Although the ruins are located on private land, efforts are being made to open this site to the public.

CAPE FEAR LIGHTHOUSE

Smith Island, North Carolina – 1903

uilt in 1903 on the southeastern tip of Smith Island, the iron-skeleton tower of Cape Fear Lighthouse stood up to many of the Atlantic's most powerful storms. It was intentionally demolished by dynamite after the station was decommissioned in 1958. Soaring nearly 160 feet above the sea, the tower's lantern held a magnificent first-order Fresnel lens suspended on a massive mercury float. Eventually, the lens was purchased by a Wilmington antiques dealer, who dismantled it and sold the prisms for five dollars each.

FEDERAL POINT LIGHT

Kure Beach, North Carolina – 1817, 1838, AND 1866

ocated on Federal Point near Wilmington, North Carolina, Fort Fisher was the site of key battles late in the Civil War. The point was once home to an array of historic lighthouses, all now destroyed. An early light tower that had stood near the fort since the 1830s was destroyed by Confederate troops in 1863. A wooden, saltbox-style lighthouse built near the ruins of the original tower served until 1881, when it was dismantled to make way for a stone breakwater.

BALD HEAD (CAPE FEAR) LIGHT

Smith Island, North Carolina — 1794 AND 1818

lthough its lantern has been dark now for nearly two thirds of a century, the Bald Head Island Lighthouse remains a majestic structure. The octagonal, brick light tower rises 110 feet above the mostly flat island, dominating the view of the Cape Fear River and the Atlantic beyond. It is not hard to understand the importance it held for generations of seamen who groped in the darkness for a safe channel into this most dangerous of rivers.

The tower retains its importance today as one of the most historic structures in North Carolina. The light station, established in 1794 on Smith Island at the mouth of the Cape Fear River, was North Carolina's first. For years the state had striven to mark the strategic cape with a lighthouse, and in 1784 the legislature levied a special tonnage tax on shipping for that purpose. The funds raised proved woefully insufficient, however, and work was not begun until 1792, after the

The lighthouse withstood an 1883 hurricane that sunk more than one hundred ships.

The massive walls of Cape Fear's "Old Baldy" race skyward in this stunning vertical photograph.

storage and work rooms stacked one atop the other. The walls tapered inward so that each of the upper rooms was smaller than the one below it.

The lantern room at the top was originally fitted with whale-oil lamps and reflectors. These were said to work well enough so that the station's fixed white light could be seen from up to 18 miles away.

Capt. Henry Hunter of the revenue cutter *Taney* inspected the station in 1834. He found it in the care of "an old Revolutionary War soldier . . . unable to give the light his constant personal attention." Presumably, the feeble warrior was soon retired or, at least, given an assistant to help him keep the oil lamps burning.

The lighthouse tower itself would eventually be an "old soldier" in need of assistance. After federal engineers closed one of the Cape Fear channels, the river current flowing past Bald Head speeded up and began to tear apart the shoreline. By the early 1880s this galloping erosion threatened the tower's foundation, and it seemed the lighthouse might suffer the same fate as its predecessor. A hastily constructed jetty slowed the current and corrected the problem just in time.

Less than a month after the jetty was completed, a hurricane roared in from the Caribbean. The storm sunk more than a hundred vessels in the Cape Fear River and along the nearby coast, but the lighthouse was spared. Since that time it has stood up to more than a century's worth of hurricanes and gales. Eventually, seamen started calling it Old Baldy.

Deactivated in 1935, the lighthouse slowly deteriorated over the decades. Since 1985, it has been maintained by a determined preservationist group called the Old Baldy Foundation. The Bald Head Lighthouse is listed on the National Register of Historic Places.

HOW TO GET THERE: *The lighthouse is located on Smith Island, which can only be reached by passenger ferry. Take State 87 or State 211 from US 17 to Southport, a quaint fishing port with lovely old homes and delightful seafood restaurants. Turn west onto West Main Street and follow the signs to the ferry landing. For ferry information or reservations, call (910) 457-5003. Ferry service is also available from Southport for visits to historic Fort Fisher and the ruins of nearby historic lighthouses. For information on the Bald Head Lighthouse, contact the Old Baldy Foundation Inc., Bald Head Island, Southport, NC 28461; (910) 457-7481.*

U.S. Congress provided for an additional $4,000. Completed at a total cost of $7,359, the lighthouse began operation in December 1796. This first Bald Head Lighthouse—referred to then as the Cape Fear Lighthouse—had a short and stormy history. Undermined by repeated gales and flood tides, it was finally knocked down by a waterspout—a coastal tornado—during the War of 1812.

In 1816 Congress appropriated $15,000 for construction of a replacement tower. Completed in 1818, the new lighthouse would prove as durable as its predecessor had proven vulnerable. It still stands, and no wonder. The tower was given fortresslike brick walls 5 feet thick at the base. It rested on a massive brick foundation 7 feet deep and covered with a thick layer of sandstone.

Unlike many light towers, the interior of the shaft was not open, but rather consisted of a series of five

OAK ISLAND LIGHT

Caswell Beach, North Carolina — 1958

Built in the late 1950s, the Oak Island Lighthouse is among the most recent and innovative of southern lighthouse towers. Constructed of reinforced concrete, the 155-foot tower looks much like a farm silo. Its builders used a moving slip-form construction technique developed in Sweden. Concrete poured into the form was allowed to dry, and then the form was moved up so that a new section could be poured. The tower never needs painting since its colors were mixed into the wet concrete. The lantern frame and floor are of lightweight aluminum. Using a powerful airport beacon, the Oak Island Light marks the entrance of North Carolina's historic Cape Fear River.

More than a century before construction of today's Oak Island tower, the Treasury Department built a pair of lighthouses on the island to mark the channel over the river bar. When sailors saw one light directly above the other, they knew they were in mid-channel. The more elevated of the two lights was mounted on a tram railway so that it could be moved whenever the channel shifted.

HOW TO GET THERE: *If approaching from south of Wilmington, take State 211 east from Supply to State 133. If driving from Wilmington, take State 87 south to State 133. When State 133 ends, continue for several miles along an unnumbered paved road. Part of the Oak Island Coast Guard Station, the lighthouse is not open to the public.*

The modern optic atop the 155-foot concrete tower can produce an extraordinary fourteen-million candlepower. Under normal conditions its flashing white light can be seen from up to 24 miles away.

ROANOKE RIVER LIGHT

Washington County, North Carolina — 1867, 1887, AND 1919

The long chain of barrier islands known as the Outer Banks shields North Carolina's intracoastal waters from the high waves and powerful storms that churn the Atlantic. As a result the Pamlico, Albermarle, and Croatan Sounds are relatively calm, and this in turn makes them inviting to mariners. From the earliest colonial times, the giant sounds were used as liquid highways for commerce. In this way they ensured the prosperity of coastal towns and farmers in eastern North Carolina, just as the Chesapeake did for settlers in the tidewater regions of Virginia and Maryland.

Also like the Chesapeake, the North Carolina sounds were once home to a sparkling array of lighthouses. Since the shallow sounds are chockablock with dangerous shallows and shoals, navigation here is tricky—and dangerous. During the nineteenth century the government built more than a dozen lighthouses in the open waters of the sounds. These guided vessels along the narrow safe channels and to busy river ports such as Morehead City, New Bern, Washington, Edenton, and Elizabeth City.

Because the sounds were shallow and their bottoms thickly layered with sand and mud, most of these lighthouses were built on pilings. Construction crews used the screw-pile technology developed earlier in the nineteenth century for use with Chesapeake Bay lighthouses. First, heavy iron pilings, each with a 3-foot-wide screw at the end, were twisted deep into the muddy bottom of the

No longer perched on its open-water screw piles, the Roanoke River Lighthouse now serves as a private cottage. The buildings and grounds are not open to the public at this time. However, a replica of this lighthouse is planned for the riverfront in downtown Plymouth, North Carolina.

This vintage photograph depicts a lighthouse tender approaching a cottage-style, screwpile light station in Pamlico Sound. The captain is keeping his hands tucked inside warm pockets while one of his crewmen readies a line. Note the sail-powered fishing boat passing on the right. (Courtesy U.S. Coast Guard)

sound. Then the firmly anchored pilings were used to hold up a platform on which a square or hexagonal wooden lighthouse was built. The completed light station would then stand like a long-legged water bug above the surface of the sound.

Most such structures had one or two stories with a small lantern perched on the roof. Usually, they encompassed no more than a thousand square feet of work and living space. On duty seven days a week for months or even years at a stretch, keepers and assistants lived full-time at the lighthouse. They tended the light, rang the station bell to warn vessels in fog or foul weather, and kept a coat of fresh white paint on the station walls so that it would serve adequately as a daymark. Often the keepers had their families with them, and all shared the same tiny, isolated world. They had no access to shore except via the station boat, which was kept on a cradle beneath the lighthouse.

Earlier in the nineteenth century, lightships marked the key channels and navigational obstacles in the Carolina sounds, but by the late 1850s these had begun to be replaced by hammered-pile or screw-pile light-

houses. From 1856 to 1891 more than a dozen pile-type lighthouses were built in North Carolina waters. Their names recall the rich maritime history of the region: Bogue Inlet, Rogue Banks, Royal Shoal, Neuse River, Brant Shoal, Olivers Reef, Pamlico Point, Long Shoal, Croatan Sound, Roanoke Marshes, Laurel Point, Wade Point, and Roanoke River.

Home to generations of keepers and their families, some of the old lighthouses served for nearly a hundred years, guiding countless ships to safe harbor. All have been removed now and replaced by pole lights or other simple markers. The last of the sound screw-pile lighthouses was discontinued and removed in 1955.

It was long thought that all these old pile-type lighthouses were burned or dismantled. Then in 1994, the incredible happened when the old Roanoke River Lighthouse was discovered safe and sound up on dry land near Edenton, North Carolina. For years the lighthouse had been used as a cottage by a private owner. Local preservationists hope to purchase the historic structure, move it to a museum or other suitable location, and open it to the public.

CHAPTER TWO

SOUTH CAROLINA:

Lights of the Southern Citadel

ecause they stand guard over key harbors and strategic points along the coast, light-houses often bear silent witness to some of history's most important events. This is especially true of the old brick and stone lighthouses along the South's Atlantic coast, many of which have stood for nearly two centuries. However, few light towers any-where have cast their long shadows over more crucial happenings than the one on Morris Island in Charleston, South Carolina.

Founded by English farmers and French Huguenots during the 1600s, Charleston is one of the old-est and most gracious cities in the South. A thriving port, Charleston was already nearly a century old by the time the first official lighthouse was built here in 1767.

Only a few years after the lighthouse was completed, the fires of revolution swept through the colonies. During the ensuing eight-year war, Charleston was captured and partially destroyed by red-coats under the command of General Cornwallis. The nearly new lighthouse was spared, probably because it served the interests of the British military as much as it did those of the colonists. But even with Charleston as a handy port for pumping redcoats and supplies into the southern colonies, the invasion that began with the conquest of Charleston in 1780 was doomed to failure. Little more than a year after it began, American independence was secured with the defeat of Cornwallis at Yorktown.

MAN-MADE EARTHQUAKE SHAKES A CITY AND A LIGHTHOUSE

As a key port in the newly independent nation, Charleston enjoyed an era of unprecedented prosper-ity, becoming the recognized center of southern culture and commerce. The Morris Island Lighthouse guided a steady stream of merchant ships to the city's wharves, where they loaded up on cotton. Unfortunately for all concerned—and to the discredit of many—some of the ships that came here brought slaves to work on the South's cotton plantations. This trade in human lives would lead to the worst catastrophe that ever struck the city.

Charleston and its lighthouse have survived many calamities. A dozen or more major hurricanes have swept over the city. In 1886 one of the most powerful earthquakes in our nation's history shook much of Charleston to its foundations—though the old light tower was left standing. But none of these natural disasters could compare with the man-made earthquake unleashed on the city in 1861 with the opening shots of the American Civil War.

Only weeks after Abraham Lincoln won the 1860 presidential election with less than a majority of the popular vote—a point some Charleston residents still consider worth making—South Carolina seceded from the Union. Seizing whatever federal property it could, the state took control of all

The historic but long abandoned Morris Island Lighthouse towers over mudflats near Charleston, South Carolina. The job of guiding ships into the city's busy harbor is now done by the much newer Sullivans Island Light, seen shining out of the mist on the left. (Courtesy Mark Riddick, New Light Photography)

This dwelling and watchtower near Charleston's Sullivans Island Lighthouse housed a sturdy lifesaving crew that raced to the rescue whenever a ship foundered nearby.

coastal lighthouses, including the one on Morris Island, and even towed the Rattlesnake Shoals Lightship into Charleston Harbor. Temporarily out of reach, however, was Fort Sumter, located on a low island a short distance from the lighthouse. Having taken refuge behind the fort's massive brick walls, a small federal force under Maj. Robert Anderson refused to surrender. For weeks Confederate artillerymen, arrayed in several batteries on the mainland, stopped reinforcements or supplies from reaching the beleaguered fort. Then, having run out of patience, they opened fire on the morning of April 12, 1861. Two days later the fort surrendered, its garrison having miraculously survived the ordeal without suffering a single casualty.

The thunder of cannon and mortar shells raining down on lightly defended Fort Sumter signaled the beginning of America's bloodiest war and of Charleston's worst nightmare. During four years of fighting, the city's defenders fought off repeated Union attacks by land and sea, holding out until the very last months of the war. Charleston might have fared better, however, had it fallen at the beginning of the war rather than at the end. During the course of the conflict, parts of the city were burned or blown up by artillery barrages, and thousands of Charlestonians died of wounds, disease, or starvation.

Snuffed out by the Confederates during the first year of fighting, the old Morris Island Light remained out of service for all but a few months of the war. The Southerners feared Union ships might follow the beacon into the harbor and attack the city. On the other hand, the light was of scant use to the Confederates, since a large federal fleet prevented all but a few blockade-running supply ships from reaching the city.

REBEL SUBMARINE MAKES HISTORY'S
FIRST TORPEDO RUN

The defenders of Charleston made numerous attempts to break the federal blockade, but none was successful. The most innovative of these came in April 1864, when the Confederates employed a tactic never before tried in the annals of naval history—a submarine torpedo attack.

For several months an experimental craft had been under development in a secret shipyard in Charleston. Only 35 feet long, it had a tube-shaped metal hull not unlike, in form at least, those of modern submarines. It had no engine, and its propeller was turned by muscular crewmen who rotated a long shaft. Designed to run just beneath the surface, it was intended to sneak up on and surprise enemy ships. As it turned out, the little vessel had a surprise in store for the Confederates as well—its nearly complete lack of seaworthiness. It proved far more effective as a watery coffin than as a warship. Every time the little submarine ventured from the dock, it promptly sank, drowning in turn each of its brave, volunteer crews. After every sinking the dogged and desperate Southerners dredged up their submarine, emptied out the seawater and the bodies, and tried again.

Perhaps reasoning that it could fare no worse in combat than it had during its trial runs, Confederate naval officials finally decided to send the submarine into battle. On the evening of April 14, 1864, it set out from Charleston bound for the federal fleet anchored just beyond the old Morris Island Lighthouse at the mouth of the harbor. Manned by yet another volunteer crew, the rebel U-boat was known as the *Hunley* after the maritime engineer who had designed it. Only a mile or so away, several large Union blockade ships waited. During the night, one of those Union warships, the *Housatonic,* blew up in a tremendous explosion that lit up the skies over Charleston. Apparently, the *Housatonic* was destroyed by the *Hunley*'s single torpedo, which had been lashed to a long spar projecting from the front of the submarine.

The Confederate submarine was not seen again for nearly a century and a half. Military historians long believed the *Hunley* had been torn apart by the powerful concussion from the torpedo attack that destroyed the *Housatonic.* During the 1990s, however, the *Hunley*'s resting place was discovered, and the historic vessel—still largely intact—was raised. Subsequent study of the wreck suggests that the *Hunley* was not sunk by the explosion, but rather by some other unknown cause. We may never know how the *Hunley* and its brave crew were lost. To learn more, visit the *Hunley,* now on display in Charleston.

A LIGHTHOUSE RISES AGAIN

After the war much of the South and Charleston lay in ruins. So, too, did the Morris Island Lighthouse. Along with more than a hundred other lighthouses along the Southern coasts, it had been darkened by the Confederates. Its huge, first-order Fresnel lens had been removed and hidden. During one of the many battles for possession of Charleston, the tower itself had been destroyed.

Reconstruction of the lighthouse did not begin until 1874. It was completed two years later during the last months of the presidency of Ulysses S. Grant. Recovered from its hiding place, the massive Fresnel lens was reinstalled atop the 155-foot tower, where it once more guided ships to Charleston. Its powerful light served far into the twentieth century and stood silent witness to the arrival of a whole new era.

Like Charleston's Morris Island Lighthouse, the light towers elsewhere along the South Carolina coast are steeped in history. In this chapter, you'll find their stories, as well as more information on the Morris Island Light.

GEORGETOWN LIGHT

Georgetown, South Carolina — 1801 AND 1812

Not long after Congress made lighthouses a federal responsibility in 1789, South Carolinians began to lobby for a light to mark the entrance to the commercially vital Winyah Bay. Although land on North Island was donated for the project by noted Revolutionary War patriot Paul Trapier, no money was available until late 1798, when Congress appropriated $7,000 to build a lighthouse.

The station was completed in early 1801, during the last days of President John Adams's administration. It consisted of a 72-foot pyramidal cypress tower; a small, two-story keeper's dwelling; and a tank for storing the whale oil that fueled the lamps. As with many such tall wooden towers, this one was unstable, and it was blown over by a gale in 1806.

The 87-foot brick tower seen here today dates to 1812, the same year the United States went to war for the second time with the British. Completed at a cost in excess of $17,000—a hefty sum at the time—the new lighthouse was built to last. It still stands today after more than 185 years.

Refurbished in 1857 when it received a fourth-order Fresnel lens and again in 1867 to repair Civil War damage, the lighthouse has served well over the years. Mariners entering Winyah Bay still watch for its white light, which flashes every fifteen seconds.

Considering its age—the Georgetown Light Station is among the oldest in the southeast—it comes as no surprise that the lighthouse is listed on the National Register of Historic Places. Nor is it surprising that the station has a resident ghost. He or she is heard occasionally walking up and down the tower's steps. Supposedly the ghost's footsteps have even been recorded on tape.

HOW TO GET THERE: *The best way to see the lighthouse is via a tour boat from Georgetown. For information or reservations write to Captain Sandy's Tours, P.O. Box 186, Georgetown, SC 29442 (843) 527–4106.*

After more than 190 years of service, the Georgetown Light still guides ships along the South Carolina coast. Some say the station is haunted.

CAPE ROMAIN LIGHT

McClellanville, South Carolina — 1827 AND 1858

Ships traveling southbound along the Carolina coasts often hug the shore to avoid the strong northeastward current of the Gulf Stream. This places them at risk of running aground on treacherous shallows that may reach several miles out into the Atlantic. Especially threatening are the shoals lurking just beneath the surface some 9 miles southeast of Cape Romain. More than a few vessels have come to grief on this formidable obstacle. To alert mariners to the danger, the government established a light station on the cape in 1827.

Well-known contractor Winslow Lewis built the first Cape Romain Lighthouse for approximately $7,500. He equipped the 65-foot conical brick tower with patent lamps and reflectors he had designed himself, billing the government an additional $950 for them. With a focal plane almost 90 feet above the water, the beacon was intended to be visible from 18 miles at sea, far enough to give ample warning of the shoals. Lewis optical systems were notoriously unreliable, however, and seamen had trouble seeing the Cape Romain beacon. Wrecks off the cape continued with monotonous—and tragic—regularity.

In 1847 the Lewis optic was replaced by a revamped system of twelve whale-oil lamps backed by a parabolic mirror almost 2 feet wide. But this new lighting apparatus also proved inadequate. An 1851 official report gave the light an unimpressive fourth-order rating. The investigating panel of lighthouse authorities who wrote the report concluded that the cape needed a much more powerful light and that a new, taller tower should be built immediately.

Completed in 1857, only a few years before the Civil War, the second Cape Romain Lighthouse owns the dubious distinction of having been built by slave labor. Even so, its octagonal brick tower is a magnificent structure soaring 150 feet into the skies above the cape. The tower's dramatic height made its light visible from at least 19 miles away. Produced by a high-quality first-order Fresnel lens, the tower's beacon was

The octagonal brick tower of the Cape Romain Light was built slightly out of plumb and its lean has never been corrected. (Courtesy U.S. Coast Guard)

first seen on January 1, 1858. The new, more powerful beacon sharply reduced the rate of shipwrecks near the cape and, no doubt, saved many lives.

Ironically, this grand tower built by slaves was nearly destroyed during the Civil War, which was fought, in part, to free slaves. Determined to put the lighthouse out of service, Confederate soldiers removed the lens and damaged the tower in 1861. Although its lantern remained dark for the rest of the war, the station was fully repaired and back in operation by 1866.

The Cape Romain tower has another curious distinction. Like the famous Leaning Tower of Pisa in Italy, it was built out of plumb. With time its foundation settled and the lighthouse leaned ever more noticeably. Eventually, the tilt became so severe that the big Fresnel lens had to be taken apart and reseated to make it work properly.

In 1931 the Fresnel was replaced by a smaller rotating bull's-eye lens. Automated in 1937, the light was discontinued ten years later. Buoys now mark the notorious shoals.

Despite its queasy lean, the Cape Romain tower has survived countless storms, including the 1989 Hurricane Hugo, which devastated much of the South Carolina coast. It still stands, as does the adjacent older tower, which was used for many years as a storage shed. Both towers are listed on the National Register of Historic Places.

HOW TO GET THERE: *The two Cape Romain lighthouses are located north of Charleston on Lighthouse Island in the Cape Romain National Wildlife Refuge, a coastal paradise of wild islands and salt marshes. The refuge and lighthouses are managed by the U.S. Fish and Wildlife Service. For information contact the Cape Romain National Wildlife Refuge, 5801 Highway 17 North, Awendaw, SC 29429; (843) 928–3368. Lighthouse Island is open to the public during the day (for safety reasons the lighthouses themselves are not) and can be reached by boat from McClellanville. For information on charters call Coastal Expeditions, Inc., at (843) 881–4582; or Captain Sandy's Tours at (843) 527–4106.*

Although the Cape Romain Lighthouse cannot bend with gale force winds like these barrier island sea oats, the tower has survived many storms including in 1989 the immensely powerful Hurricane Hugo.

CHARLESTON LIGHTHOUSE

Sullivans Island, South Carolina — 1962

Among the oldest and most gracious cities in America, Charleston, South Carolina, was the site of one of the earliest lighthouses on this continent. Charleston's original Morris Island Light Station was established in 1767. So it is ironic that Charleston is now served by one of the nation's most thoroughly modern light towers.

Unlike the old Morris Island Station, which predates the Revolution, the Charleston Light, on Sullivans Island near Fort Moultrie, is a product of the rock 'n' roll era. Whereas the tower on Morris Island was a traditional conical structure built of brick and stone, the Sullivans Island tower is triangular and fashioned of reinforced concrete clad in aluminum siding.

Completed in 1962, the Charleston Light tower is 140 feet tall, placing the elevation of its light a lofty 163 feet above sea level. Old-time keepers trudged up spiral steps to tend the oil lamps of their lighthouses. Should anyone need to check the automated lighting apparatus atop the giant tower on Sullivans Island, they are whisked to the lantern room in a lift—the only lighthouse elevator in the United States.

Coast Guard personnel who occasionally visit the lantern room for routine maintenance must use extreme caution to avoid burns and eye damage. The station's optic can generate a sizzling twenty-eight million candlepower. The flashing white beacon can be seen from up to 26 miles at sea. The light marks the entrance to Charleston Harbor.

HOW TO GET THERE: *From Charleston follow US 17 and then State 703 to Mount Pleasant. Cross the Sawyer Memorial Bridge to Sullivans Island and follow the signs toward Fort Moultrie. As you approach the fort, you'll see the tower on the left about 2 blocks off Middle Street. The tower is closed to the public, but visitors are welcome to walk the station grounds.*

While in the area be sure to visit Fort Moultrie National Monument. The fort took part in Revolutionary War and Civil War battles. Edgar Allan Poe was once stationed here, and so, interestingly enough, was William Sherman. It is said Sherman enjoyed the time he spent at Moultrie during the years before the Civil War and that he grew to love the Old South, which, as Union Army General Sherman, he would later do so much to destroy. For more information on Fort Moultrie National Monument, call (843) 883–3123.

The modern-looking triangular tower of the Charleston Lighthouse on Sullivans Island houses an optic of extraordinary power.

MORRIS ISLAND LIGHT

Morris Island, South Carolina – 1767, 1837, AND 1876

Acopper plate inserted in the cornerstone of the Charleston Lighthouse reads, THE FIRST STONE OF THIS BEACON WAS LAID ON THE 30TH OF MAY 1767 IN THE SEVENTH YEAR OF HIS MAJESTY'S REIGN, GEORGE THE III. Built by the British colony of South Carolina a few years after the conclusion of the French and Indian War, the Charleston Lighthouse was for decades the only significant navigational light on the southern coasts of America. Located on Morris Island at the entrance to Charleston Harbor, the lighthouse guided ships first with beacons of burning pitch and oakum, then large tallow candles, and later spider lamps.

With the passage of the Lighthouse Act, among the first measures enacted by Congress under the Constitution, the federal government inherited the Charleston Lighthouse. In 1800 Congress spent $5,000—a princely sum in that day—repairing and fitting it with an updated lighting apparatus. But by 1837 the old lighthouse had been replaced by a tower built on what was then called Lighthouse Island. The new tower, not far from Fort Sumter, stood 102 feet from base to lantern and had a revolving light. It received a first-order Fresnel lens in 1858, less than three years before the outbreak of the Civil War.

In April of 1861, with war on the horizon, the governor of secessionist South Carolina demanded that the federal government surrender the lighthouse along with all other markers and buoys in the harbor. The board gave up the Charleston Light without a fight, but President Lincoln refused to order his troops to abandon nearby Fort Sumter. As a result, the first battle of the fratricidal "War Between the States" was fought practically in the shadow of the Charleston Lighthouse. The Confederates of South Carolina won the battle, forcing Union troops at Fort Sumter to strike their colors.

The Confederates held Charleston for most of the war, but they could not control the seas beyond the city's once busy harbor. The U.S. Navy imposed a tight blockade, and not long after the fall of Sumter, a Union fleet followed the lighthouse beacon into the Charleston Harbor in an effort to take the city by sea. The attacking fleet was driven off by artillery at Fort Wagner and Fort Gregg, both located on Lighthouse

The sandy island under Charleston Lighthouse has all but disappeared. The copper plate on the base says the tower's cornerstone was laid in 1767. (Courtesy U.S. Coast Guard)

Island. Soon after the attack, the Confederates darkened the light.

When federal forces finally captured Charleston by land invasion in 1865, they discovered that the Charleston Lighthouse tower had been destroyed. The Lighthouse Board soon learned that the neglected harbor itself had also suffered damage in the war: old channels had been silted over and new ones had been opened up by the tides. To guide ships effectively through the radically altered channels, a new light was needed. After some years of indecision, the board let a contract for a lighthouse to be built on the site of the old colonial tower.

Begun in 1874, the new tower took two years to build. Workmen drove piles 50 feet into the mud beneath the island, pouring onto them an 8-foot-thick concrete foundation, and on this solid base, they raised a brick tower 161 feet high. The lighthouse, placed in service on October 1, 1876, was indeed well built. It survived a major hurricane in 1885 and the following year, an earthquake, which devastated much of Charleston.

Sometime prior to 1892, the tower was painted black with white bands to make it easier to use as a daymark. Charleston Light on Morris Island was replaced in 1962 by a new lighthouse on Sullivans Island. The Coast Guard planned to tear down the old tower, but a local citizens group, led by the son of a former Charleston Lighthouse keeper, fought successfully to preserve the structure.

However, their efforts came too late to save the station's fine old first-order Fresnel lens. Incredibly, it was sold at auction just as if it had been an antique chandelier taken from some old dilapidated mansion in the city's historic district. Even the tower itself was sold to salvagers, but the Preservation Society of Charleston stepped in just in time to stop the wrecking cranes.

While the hard-working society members managed to save the lighthouse from man-made destruction, they could not hold back the sea. In 1896, the government built a jetty to stop erosion of Morris Island. It had the opposite effect and, before long, the island disappeared altogether. Nothing remains of it today but an expanse of mudflats.

Although this grand old lighthouse may yet succumb to the sea, vigorous efforts are now under way to save it. In 2001 the property was given government protection by transferring ownership to the state of South Carolina. Nearly $1 million in state and private funding has been raised to restore the tower. Soon, the Army Corps of Engineers may attempt to rebuild part of the island that once protected the tower's foundation from the tides.

HOW TO GET THERE: *Take US 17 south from Charleston. After crossing the Ashley River, turn left onto State 171 and follow it to Folley Beach. About a block before State 171 ends at the Atlantic Ocean, turn left onto East Ashley Street and follow it for several miles until it ends at the gate to the U.S. Coast Guard station. Leave your car in the parking area about 100 yards from the gate and follow the path over the dunes to the beach. The lighthouse stands about a quarter mile north on a sandbar separated from the island by erosion.*

HUNTING ISLAND LIGHT

Hunting Island State Park, South Carolina — 1859 AND 1875

The Lighthouse Board had a tower constructed on Hunting Island, about halfway between Charleston and Savannah, in 1859. During the Civil War, the Hunting Island Light went dark along with most of the other Southern lights, and by the end of the war the tower had mysteriously disappeared. No one knows for sure whether the tower was destroyed by the Confederates or was so badly undermined by erosion that it fell into the sea.

In 1875 another tower was built within a mile of the original light station. Constructed of interchangeable cast-iron sections that could be dismantled and reassembled when necessary, the 95-foot tower was lined with bricks. A three-story keeper's house, an oil house, and several outbuildings stood near the tower.

All of these structures were soon threatened by the sea. Gnawing continuously at the land, the waves moved to within 150 feet of the tower and only 60 feet from the keeper's dwelling by 1887. When a series of jetties and revetments failed to stop the advancing water, the board decided to move the station. In 1889 the cast-iron tower was dismantled and rebuilt more than a mile inland.

The light, which is no longer in service, had a second-order Fresnel lens and could be seen from 18 miles away. The top of the tower is 136 feet from the ground and is reached by a staircase of 181 steps.

HOW TO GET THERE: *Take US 21 east from Beaufort to Hunting Island State Park. A paved road, curving through the island's maritime forest, leads to the lighthouse. Several original outbuildings—probably used for storing oil and other supplies—are still intact. The magnificent first-order Fresnel lens from the Morris Island Lighthouse, better known as the old Charleston Light, is on display at the Hunting Island Lighthouse. Restoration was completed at Hunting Island in spring 1994, and the lighthouse is now open seven days a week from Memorial Day through Labor Day and other times by appointment; call (843) 838–2011. Visitors may climb the old lighthouse stairs and enjoy the view. For more information write Hunting Island State Park, 2555 Sea Island Parkway, Hunting Island, SC 29920.*

The black upper section of the Hunting Island Lighthouse seems to float in the sky when seen against a bank of white clouds. Its light extinguished in 1933, the tower is now used only as a daymark.

HILTON HEAD REAR RANGE LIGHT
Hilton Head Island, South Carolina — 1881

irst marked during the Civil War by a Union Navy lightship, Hilton Head received its first official light station in 1881. The station displayed two lights, one of them shining from the lantern room of a tall skeleton tower, the other from a lesser tower perched atop a house. Located about a mile from one another, these two range lights lined up to mark a safe channel for approaching vessels (see the Daufuskie Island section for more information on range lights).

To help it withstand gales, the 95-foot rear range tower was built on braced iron legs. Keepers reached its lantern room by climbing the 112-step spiral staircase winding upward through a central steel cylinder. The hexagonal wooden lantern room once held a Fresnel lens. Oil or kerosene lamps provided the light, which could be seen from about 15 miles away. The smaller front range lighthouse was constructed in such a way that it could be moved from place to place as shifting sands clogged the channel and forced realignment of the lights. Both lights were taken out of service in 1932.

A pair of keeper's dwellings built near the rear range tower during the late 1800s were said to be haunted. According to popular legend, the ghost is that of Caroline Fripp, the daughter of an early keeper.

When a giant hurricane hit the island in 1898, keeper Adam Fripp, a widower, hurried up the steps of the lighthouse to tend the lamps. Close at his heels was his twenty-year-old-daughter, Caroline, who wore a long blue dress. At the height of the storm, an explosive gust of wind blew out the glass in the lantern, extinguishing the lamps. At this critical moment, the keeper was struck by a fatal heart attack.

Although dying, Fripp urged his daughter to relight the lamps. He admonished her to keep them burning, and this she did all through the night of the storm and several nights thereafter. But Caroline never recovered from the strain of those long, lonely nights nor from the grief she suffered over the death of her father. She died about three weeks later.

Over the years, residents and visitors to Hilton Head Island have reported occasional sightings of a ghostly female figure in a blue dress. There have also been reports of mysterious wails and sobbing heard in the vicinity of the now-abandoned lighthouse and of the keeper's dwellings, now moved to Harbour Town.

HOW TO GET THERE: *The skeleton tower that once displayed the Hilton Head Station's rear range light still stands; it is located in the exclusive Palmetto Dunes resort complex on Hilton Head Island. Palmetto Dunes is closed to the public except by invitation or permission; call (800) 845–8001.*

The haunted keeper's dwellings have been moved to Harbour Town in Sea Pines Plantation. Also at Harbour Town is a red-and-white-striped 90-foot light tower with a gift shop and small flashing optic at the top. For information contact Sea Pines Resort, P.O. Box 7000, Hilton Head Island, SC 29928; (843) 785–3333.

The steel tower of the Hilton Head Rear Range Light now graces a posh coastal golf resort.

HARBOUR TOWN LIGHT
Hilton Head Island, South Carolina — 1970

The 90-foot, red-and-white-striped tower of the Harbour Town Lighthouse is the visual centerpiece of the popular Sea Pines on Hilton Head Island. Its light flashes white every two and a half seconds and helps mark the Inland Waterway and Calibogue Sound. Completed in 1970, this was the first privately financed light tower to be built since the early 1800s. Visitors who climb the tower steps will find an excellent spot from which to view Hilton Head.

DAUFUSKIE ISLAND RANGE LIGHTS:

BLOODY POINT REAR RANGE LIGHT
Freeport, South Carolina — EARLY 1800S AND 1883

HAIG POINT REAR RANGE LIGHT
Freeport, South Carolina — 1872 AND 1986

So many battles were fought on Daufuskie Island that locals came to call it the "Place of Blood." The Native Americans who once inhabited the island fiercely defended it against repeated invasions by pirates, Spanish soldiers, and English settlers. Eventually, the island's Native American defenders were overwhelmed and exterminated while making a last stand against the British at a place now known as Bloody Point.

The island's rich, blood-drenched soil eventually gave rise to prosperous plantations, attracting frequent visits from merchant ships that came here to load up with cotton, rice, and sugar. During the harvest season, these vessels regularly sailed past Bloody Point. Likely ignorant of its dark past, the masters of ships approaching the point at night often saw something bright and reassuring there—a pair of lights arranged to guide them safely into nearby Calibogue Sound.

From this angle, the Haig Point Lighthouse on bucolic Daufuskie Island suggests a church and steeple. The building is now used as a private club. (Courtesy Daniel J. Gruszka)

Bloody Point was the site of one of America's earliest pair of range lights. A candle displayed in the attic window of a house that once stood on the point served as the rear range light. The front range light shone from a pole just off the beach. When observed from mid-channel, the two lights could be seen one above the other and perpendicular to the water. When the upper light appeared to tilt left or right, a captain knew his vessel had veered out of the safe channel and would correct his course by steering in the direction of the tilt.

Established during the early 1800s, the Bloody Point Range Lights guided mariners for more than a century. In time the candles were replaced by kerosene lanterns, and then by electric bulbs. The lights were finally extinguished in 1922. The building that once served as the Bloody Point Rear Range Lighthouse still stands but has been moved away from the water.

For more than half a century, Daufuskie Island was home to not one but two sets of range lights. Beginning in 1872 a second pair marked the island's Haig Point and guided ships into the broad Cooper River. The Haig Point front range light was set on a pole far out in the water, while the rear range light shone from a 25-foot-tall tower atop the keeper's dwelling. For many years the rear range beacon was provided by a fifth-order Fresnel lens, lighted by a kerosene lamp—electricity was a relative latecomer to this remote island.

The government deactivated the Haig Point Range Lights in 1934. Eventually, the boarded-up Victorian dwelling and rear range tower were purchased by the International Paper Company and became the home of the private Haig Point Club. The lighthouse serves club members as a bed-and-breakfast and restaurant. In 1986 the rear range light was restored as a private aid to navigation. The Haig Point Rear Range Lighthouse is listed on the National Register of Historic Places.

Today Daufuskie Island is seen by many as a sort of time capsule. The so-called Gullah people who still live here are the descendants of plantation slaves freed after the Civil War. Because of their isolation on Daufuskie and similar remote islands along the Carolina, Georgia, and Florida coasts, their culture and dialect have been handed down more or less intact from the antebellum era. The extraordinary Gullah language contains many African words.

As a young man, author Pat Conroy taught school on Daufuskie Island, and the experience became the model for his novel *The Water Is Wide* as well as for the movie *Conrack*. The movie and novel did much to open Daufuskie Island and its people to the outside world.

HOW TO GET THERE: *Daufuskie Island can be reached via scheduled cruises from Hilton Head. Contact Adventure Cruises, Shelter Cove Harbour, Hilton Head Island, SC 29928; (843) 785–4558. The Safari Cruise stops at Daufuskie, allowing passengers to tour the island by bus or golf cart and get close-up views of the two old rear range lighthouses.*

The keeper and his family pose for a late nineteenth-century photograph of the Haig Point Lighthouse. (Courtesy U.S. Coast Guard)

CHAPTER THREE

GEORGIA:
Lights of the Grass Seas

irst-time visitors to the Georgia coast may quickly conclude that this is a region unable to decide whether it is part of the land or of the ocean. A gap of several miles separates Georgia's nearly continuous wall of barrier islands from the dry mainland. The area between is filled with a wriggling mass of crisscrossing inlets and seas of tall marsh grasses that often extend to the horizon. Beneath the grass is a layer of dense mud deep enough to swallow a ship or even a whole town. In fact, more than a few of the state's early coastal towns simply disappeared into the muck. One that did not was Savannah, founded along with the new colony of Georgia by Gen. James Oglethorpe in 1733. (Georgia was the last of the original thirteen American colonies to be settled.)

Located several miles from the Atlantic on the banks of the sizable river that bears its name, Savannah gave the new colony a vital link to the ocean and the world beyond. Recognizing its strategic importance, Oglethorpe had his troops build a tower to mark the entrance to the Savannah River. Completed on Tybee Island in 1736, the 90-foot brick-and-cedar tower served as an unlighted daymark and military watch post. The tower was soon destroyed by storms, but Oglethorpe had it rebuilt before hurrying south to turn back a Spanish invasion at the Battle of Bloody Marsh. (The Spanish got stuck in the mud.)

Repaired or rebuilt several times over the years, the tower eventually received a light to guide ships into the river at night. The actual date the tower was first lighted has been lost in the mists of history, but by the 1770s and the outbreak of the Revolutionary War, Tybee was known to sea captains as one of only a handful of reliable navigational lights along the entire Atlantic coast. It would remain in continuous operation right up until the Civil War, when it was darkened by the Confederates. Restored after the war, the old lighthouse remains in service to this day.

BRICK WALLS VERSUS RIFLED CANNON

During the late 1840s a pair of lights was placed on two small islands to guide vessels through channels on the north and south sides of the river and into the Savannah harbor. One of these, the North Channel Light, stood on an exposed outcropping of white oyster beds. This tenuous bit of "land" has long since disappeared along with the small brick lighthouse tower it once supported. The South Channel Light, however, still stands. Established on Cockspur Island in 1848, it served mariners for more than a century. The survival of this little 35-foot tower was a near miracle, considering that it was caught in the middle of one of history's fiercest artillery barrages.

In the spring of 1862, Union troops placed several batteries of heavy guns on Tybee Island. Their target was to be the Confederate stronghold at Fort Pulaski, about a mile away. The lighthouse, which had been darkened during the early days of the war, stood in the line of fire between the two forces.

Two powerful and long-lived symbols—Old Glory flutters in front of the gleaming white St. Simons tower. The lighthouse has survived more than a century, and the nation, of course, more than two centuries.

Land and water trade places frequently in coastal Georgia. Nowadays, the shell beds and marsh grasses stop well short of the Cockspur Lighthouse, which once stood on an island.

The firing began on the night of April 11, when federal gunners opened up on the fort.

At first the Confederates at Pulaski felt they had little to fear from the Union guns. Theirs was one of the stoutest bastions ever built. Completed during the 1840s at a cost of more than a million dollars, the fort featured 7-foot-thick walls that contained twenty-five million bricks and were believed capable of withstanding anything an enemy could throw at them.

What the defenders did not know was that the federal artillerymen facing them possessed an experimental weapon. The new, rifled Parrot guns in the Union batteries proved so powerful that they could drive their thirty-six-pound shot almost 2 feet into Pulaski's brick walls. More than 5,000 of these shot were fired, and they chipped, cracked, and blasted the masonry until the walls started to fall apart. Union shells began to pass through the gaping holes and strike the walls of the magazine, where 40,000 pounds of gunpowder were stored. Realizing that sooner or later an explosive shell would penetrate the magazine, blowing the fort and its garrison to kingdom come, the Southerners surrendered.

Only one Southern soldier was killed during the bombardment. The Cockspur Island Lighthouse, which had seemed in mortal danger, emerged from the battle unscathed. Ironically, the lighthouse survived because the Union Parrot guns turned out to be not only more powerful, but much more accurate, than earlier types of ordnance. Had old-fashioned cannon been used to fire on the fort, stray shots would most certainly have battered down the little tower.

The loss of Pulaski and forts like it all along the Southern coast spelled doom for the Confederacy.

Together with its overwhelming naval strength, possession of key forts such as Pulaski enabled the Union to bottle up Southern ports and block the import of badly need munitions and supplies. Few nations can survive long without foreign trade, let alone one where the primary industries are, as Rhett Butler put it in Margaret Mitchell's classic *Gone with the Wind,* "cotton, sugar cane, and arrogance." The plight of the blockaded South during the Civil War indirectly illustrates the vital importance of lighthouses. They helped open the country to seaborne commerce by breaking what would otherwise have been a natural blockade of dangerous navigational obstacles and darkness.

GONE OVER THE WAVES

Savannah has its own Scarlett and Rhett love story. This one concerns Florence Martus, the sister of George W. Martus, who served for many years as keeper of Cockspur Island Light. For most of her life, Florence lived with her brother in a cottage on nearby Elba Island. One fine day in 1887, several sailors, whose ship had docked at Savannah, rowed across to Fort Pulaski, where Florence was spending the afternoon with her father. Florence's father, who had fought at Pulaski, offered to give the sailors a tour of the island. While her father reminisced about his Civil War days, Florence caught the eye of one of the seamen.

A handsome young man, the sailor asked if he could call on her. She agreed. He visited Florence three times while his ship was in port, and before he left, he promised to return and marry her.

"I'll wait for you always," she told him. As his ship sailed with the high tide on the morning following their last meeting, Florence stood in front of her cottage and waved a white handkerchief. No one knows if the sailor waved back at her.

Florence's sailor never returned, and for more than fifty years she continued to wave in vain at every passing ship. But having lost the love of a particular seaman, she won the hearts of mariners in general. Every year more and more sailors watched for her handkerchief as they passed her cottage. Often they brought her gifts from distant ports they had visited. One sailor even brought her a llama from Peru.

Fireworks compete with a full moon and the bright Tybee Island beacon during a 1999 spectacular celebrating completion of restoration work at the historic light station. Like many historic lighthouses, this one fell on hard times after it was automated in 1972, but a determined group of preservationists helped save it.

COCKSPUR ISLAND LIGHT

Cockspur Island, Georgia — CA. 1848

The Cockspur Island Light, also known as the South Channel Light, was lit in 1848 along with its companion, the North Channel Light. The two lights guided ships up the Savannah River past Tybee Island, around Elba and Cockspur Islands, into Savannah, Georgia.

Like most lights along the Southern coasts, these two lighthouses were darkened by the Civil War. The North Channel Light, built on Oyster Bed Island, did not survive the fighting. But the South Channel Light, located at the eastern end of Cockspur Island, proved luckier. Although it stood in the direct line of fire during the terrific artillery duel between Confederate batteries at Fort Pulaski and the big Union guns on Tybee Island, the South Channel Light escaped the battle without a scratch.

The Cockspur Island Light was relit following the war and continued in service until 1949, when it was permanently retired. After several years of neglect, the lighthouse was deeded to the National Park Service. Restored in 1978, it is now open to the public.

HOW TO GET THERE: *Take US 80 east from Savannah. The tower can be seen from the US 80 bridge. The lighthouse stands on an oyster bed off Tybee Island, and the adventuresome can reach it by wading or swimming, depending on the tide. The Park Service, however, recommends renting a boat.*

Historic Fort Pulaski, completed in 1848, is well worth a visit. The brick-and-stone fort took eighteen years to build but only a few days to fall to Union forces during an 1862 artillery duel. The fort's brick walls could not stand up to the Union gunners' rifled cannon. For information contact Pulaski National Monument, P.O. Box 30757, Savannah, GA 31410; (912) 786–5787.

Although Cockspur Island has all but disappeared beneath the waters of the Savannah River estuary, the National Park Service hopes to save the historic light tower that has stood here since 1848.

TYBEE ISLAND LIGHT

Tybee Island, Georgia — 1791, 1857, AND 1867

ocated at the mouth of the Savannah River in Georgia, the Tybee Island Light was among the first of the South's great lighthouses. Gen. James Oglethorpe commissioned a navigational marker for the commercially strategic river mouth soon after he established the colony of Georgia in 1733. On orders from Oglethorpe, William Blytheman built a 90-foot, octagonal tower of wood on Tybee Island in 1736. The wood-frame tower could not stand up to the power of ocean gales, and in 1741 a storm knocked it down.

The smashed marker was replaced in 1742 by a second wooden tower, this one 94 feet tall and topped by a 30-foot flagpole. In 1768 this tower also fell to the wind and sea, and a third was constructed in 1773. Intended only as daymarks, none of the early Tybee towers displayed a light.

The federal government took possession of the Tybee marker in 1791 and for the first time fitted it with a lamp. The keeper used candles for the light, as was the practice in most lighthouses at that time. Flame and wood, however, are a dangerous combination, and only about a year after Tybee began to display its light, the wooden structure was damaged by fire. Savannah customs inspector Jesse Tay happened to be on hand when the fire broke out, and he later described the disaster in the following quaint language: "i jumped up and run up Stairs . . . the glass and sinders was fawling so thick and it was so very hot i was not able to tarry half a moment and i saw it was in vain to attempt to save it."

Rebuilt, this time with brick instead of wood, the tower was fitted with Winslow Lewis's lamps and reflectors. The Lewis system employed a smokeless, hollow-wicked oil lamp of a type invented by Ami Argond in 1781. The Argond lamp allowed air to flow freely around and through the wick, thus producing a bright light equal to that of seven candles. Lewis placed the lamp at the center of a large parabolic reflector, which intensified and focused the light. In 1822 a second, shorter tower was built some distance from the main lighthouse. Pilots who saw the two lights vertically aligned one atop the other knew their ships were in mid-channel. In 1857 the main tower was raised to 100 feet and fitted with a second-order Fresnel lens.

The renovated lighthouse had been in use for only

The navigational station at Tybee Island dates back to colonial times. These marchers honor the station's extraordinary history by displaying the flags that have flown over the island since James Oglethorpe founded Georgia in the 1730s.

Rebuilt after it was burned by Confederate troops during the Civil War, the Tybee Island Lighthouse has guided countless vessels to Savannah. Now it brings tourists here as well.

order Fresnel lens, it projected a beam visible from almost 20 miles at sea.

In 1871 and again in 1878, Tybee was hit with storms so powerful that they cracked the tower. Then, in 1886, an earthquake lengthened the cracks and broke the lens. A Lighthouse Board inspector noted: "The earthquake of last August extended the cracks that have been observed in this tower for several years and made some new ones. . . . The lens was displaced and the attachments to its upper ring were broken."

The board concluded that the tower must be rebuilt, but Congress refused to provide the funds. Consequently, the old tower still stands today, looking much as it did just after the Civil War. Substantial restoration work has been done on the tower. It has been repainted, returning it to the original black-white-black color configuration.

The Tybee Museum exhibits artifacts and other memorabilia of Tybee from the seventeenth century through World War II. A submarine periscope allows visitors to view the beach and lighthouse from inside the museum.

HOW TO GET THERE: *Take US 80 east from Savannah to Tybee Island. The lighthouse, which can be seen from several miles away, is at the north end of the island in old Fort Screven. The tower can be climbed for breathtaking views of the Atlantic, the Savannah River, the ruins of Fort Screven, and the Victorian homes on Officer's Row. There is a museum at the fort. There is an admission fee for the lighthouse and museum. The lighthouse is open from 10:00 A.M. to 6:00 P.M. daily during the summer; from Labor Day to April, it is open 12:00 to 4:00 P.M. weekdays and 10:00 A.M. to 4:00 P.M. weekends. For more information contact the Tybee Island Lighthouse and Museum, P.O. Box 366, Tybee Island, GA 31328; (912) 786–5801.*

about five years when the Union Army invaded Tybee Island and used it as a staging area for attacks on the Confederates at nearby Fort Pulaski. As they retreated, the Confederates set the lighthouse on fire, putting it out of service for the duration of the Civil War.

Federal troops attempted to restore the fire-gutted tower, but an outbreak of cholera hampered the effort. Work ceased altogether when the foreman and four workers died of the disease. As a result, the restoration was not finished until nearly two years after the war. When the work was at last complete and the lamps relit on October 1, 1867, the brick Tybee Island tower reached 154 feet above sea level. Fitted with a first-

SAPELO ISLAND LIGHT

Sapelo Island, Georgia — 1820

ew places along the East Coast of the United States are as wild as Georgia's Sapelo Island, a natural treasure trove of tall marsh grass, pristine beaches, and gnarled coastal forests. The incredibly rich soils here made antebellum plantation owners rich, but following the Civil War, the island returned to nature. Except for a handful of lighthouse keepers and a small community of Gullah people, descended from the slaves who once worked the island's sugarcane and cotton fields, it has remained uninhabited for more than a century.

The first Sapelo Island light tower was the work of Winslow Lewis, who built so many of America's early lighthouses. By 1820 Lewis had completed an 80-foot brick-and-stone tower and accompanying keeper's dwelling. For his trouble and expenses, Lewis billed the government approximately $17,000—quite a substantial sum at the time. The price included the lighting apparatus, a patent lamp and reflector arrangement Lewis had designed himself.

During the early 1850s the government upgraded the Sapelo Island facility—along with most other U.S. lighthouses—raising the tower by 10 feet and installing a fourth-order Fresnel lens. Following severe storm damage in 1867, the tower received extensive repairs and restoration.

Early in the twentieth century lighthouse officials decided to build a new lighthouse on Sapelo Island. Just over 100 feet tall, the tower was of a steel-skeleton design intended to resist the high winds generated by gales and hurricanes. Completed in 1905, it served without serious incident until 1933, when it was deactivated. Several years later the tower was dismantled and shipped to Lake Superior for use in the Apostle Islands.

HOW TO GET THERE: *Few lighthouses are more remote or harder to visit than those on Georgia's*

Sapelo Island. *The Georgia Department of Natural Resources maintains the island as a wildlife and nature preserve. Lighthouse tours are available through Southeast Adventure Outfitters. Tour boats leave the Meridian, Georgia, boat landing nearly every morning. Advance reservations are required. For information or reservations contact Southeast Adventure Outfitters, 313 Mallory Street, St. Simons Island, GA 31522; (912) 638–6732. For more information on the state-run nature tours of Sapelo Island, call (912) 437–3224.*

Deactivated in 1899, the Sapelo Island Lighthouse stood empty and abandoned for a century. Restored by the state in 1999, the station has returned to duty as an active aid to navigation.

ST. SIMONS ISLAND LIGHT

St. Simons Island, Georgia — CA. 1810 AND 1872

ighthouse keepers and their assistants were not always the closest of friends. One Sunday morning in March 1880, the St. Simons lighthouse keeper fought with his assistant keeper on the front lawn of the lighthouse, and the assistant shot his superior dead. The assistant, who was relieved of his duties, was later acquitted of murder charges.

In 1907 Carl Svendsen, his wife, and their dog, Jinx, moved to the then–almost deserted island to tend the light. The Svendsens happily went about their profes-

sional and domestic business, unaware of the death that had taken place there twenty-seven years earlier. Mrs. Svendsen always waited for her husband to clamber down the tower stairs from the light room before she laid dinner on the table. One evening, hearing a heavy tread on the steps, she put out the food as usual. But this time, when the shoes reached the bottom step, her husband did not appear. Jinx barked an alarm and then scampered for safety.

Mrs. Svendsen climbed the lighthouse steps to look for her husband and found him still at the top of the tower. She told him what she had heard, and at first, Svendsen feared his wife had gone daft in the isolation of their lighthouse station. Then, a few days later, he himself heard the phantom footsteps.

The Svendsens lived in the house for twenty-eight years without ever finding an explanation for the bodiless footsteps that never failed to send Jinx into a frenzy.

The original lighthouse was built in 1810 at the southern extremity of St. Simons Island east of Brunswick, Georgia, to mark the St. Simons Sound. Constructed of tabby, the tower was a white, tapered octagonal structure 75 feet tall. It was topped by a 10-foot iron lantern lit by oil lamps held in suspension by chains. Serving first as a harbor light, it was raised to the status of a coastal light in 1857 when the Lighthouse Board installed a third-order Fresnel lens.

The tower and all the light-station outbuildings were destroyed by Confederate troops in 1862 as they retreated from the island. Following the war, the board let a contract to build a new station with a 106-foot tower. As was the case with the building of many southern lighthouses, a mysterious sickness—probably malaria—plagued the construction crew. The contractor himself fell ill and died in 1870. One of the bondsmen took charge of construction in order to protect his investment, but he, too, fell victim to illness shortly after his arrival. Despite the lives lost during construction of the St. Simons Light Station, the tower was completed by a second bondsman, and the lamps were lit on September 1, 1872. The new tower, painted white, had a focal plane 106 feet above sea level.

The St. Simons Island Lighthouse remains in service

to this day, and its third-order, L. Sautter Company Fresnel lens is still in place. The beacon flashes white once every minute and can be seen from more than 20 miles away. The light station has been listed on the National Register of Historic Places since 1972.

HOW TO GET THERE: *Take the St. Simons Island causeway east from Brunswick; once on the island, take Kings Way to the south end of the island. The lighthouse is located at the end of Kings Way, which turns into Beachview. Take Beachview and turn right onto Twelfth Street. The lighthouse is 2 blocks down on the left, with a shopping area and post office*

nearby. The white tapering tower and the classic keeper's house are some of the best examples of American lighthouse architecture in the South.

There is a small parking area close to the front door of the keeper's quarters, which houses the Museum of Coastal History. There is an admission fee for both the museum and the lighthouse. The climb to the top of the 106-foot-tall tower provides a grand view of the island.

The lighthouse and museum are open daily except Monday and some major holidays. Call (912) 638–4666 for more information or to arrange a tour.

The St. Simons Island keeper's house, now a museum of coastal history, was built during the grand period of lighthouse construction in the South after the Civil War.

LITTLE CUMBERLAND ISLAND LIGHT

Little Cumberland Island, Georgia — 1820 AND 1838

Winslow Lewis, America's most prolific lighthouse builder, received a contract in 1819 to erect a light tower and dwelling on Georgia's Little Cumberland Island. As with the Sapelo Island Light Station farther up the coast, Lewis was to receive $17,000 for the project. For this the contractor provided the station with a 50-foot brick tower, a small brick keeper's dwelling, and a lighting apparatus for the lantern.

Lewis had the Little Cumberland Island Station ready for service in less than one year, and its lamps were first lit on Independence Day in 1820. Like other Lewis towers, this one employed the lamp-and-reflector system he had invented himself.

In 1838 lighthouse officials decided to build a new tower on Little Cumberland Island's northernmost point. (The original station stood on the south end of the island.) While the new lighthouse was under construction, the old one was taken apart brick by brick, shipped to Florida, and reassembled on Amelia Island, where it still stands today.

The new 60-foot tower was given brick walls supported by heavy cross-timbers. Inevitably, given the island's hot and damp climate, the timbers rotted. Eventually, they were replaced with iron braces.

In 1857 a sparkling, third-order Fresnel lens, manufactured in Paris by the well-known Henri LePaute firm, supplanted the old Lewis-style lamps-and-reflector optic. During the Civil War Confederate troops damaged the lens and the tower, putting the station out of service until repairs could be completed in 1867. The station was discontinued and abandoned in 1915.

The private Little Cumberland Island Association acquired the lighthouse in 1967. The association found the tower to be in remarkably good shape, even after more than half a century of disuse and neglect. Periodic restorations have left the historic tower in excellent condition. Today it is listed on the National Register of Historic Places.

Coastal oaks lay siege to the Little Cumberland Island Lighthouse. A private association maintains the unused tower. (Courtesy Bob and Sandra Shanklin)

HOW TO GET THERE: *Little Cumberland Island is a private residential community, and neither the island nor the lighthouse is open to the public. However, tour cruises from nearby Jekyll Island pass within sight of the tower. For information contact Coastal Expeditions, 3202 East Third Street, Brunswick, GA 31520; (912) 265–0392.*

CHAPTER FOUR

FLORIDA:

Lights of the Hurricane Peninsula

By the nineteenth century the Florida peninsula, together with the chain of low, sandy islands (known as keys) extending westward from its southern tip, was well established as the world's most formidable navigational obstacle. Countless ships and untold thousands of lives had been lost to its shoals and unmarked headlands. Although entire Spanish fleets were wiped out in storm-driven collisions with the Florida coast, there is no clear evidence that the Spanish ever erected any lighthouses there.

But the United States, which took possession of Florida in 1821, could not afford to be as lax as the Spanish had been in the matter of lighthouse construction. Following the Louisiana Purchase in 1803, the seas around Florida had become the young nation's busiest highway for commerce. Since the great wall of the Appalachian Mountains divided the rich farm and cattle lands of the Mississippi Basin from the populous cities of the East Coast, western produce had to be shipped to market by sea. Timber, grain, and livestock were floated down the big muddy western rivers in flatboats to New Orleans and other ports and then loaded onto sailing vessels for the journey eastward to the U.S. Atlantic coast or to Europe.

The voyage invariably took merchant ships around the southern tip of Florida, and every year the treacherous Florida coasts exacted a heavy toll of ships, crews, and cargoes. Wrecks occurred with such regularity that salvaging lost cargo grew into a major industry. A thriving town, almost entirely supported by the salvaging business, took root on Key West. There, dozens of salvaging crews, called "wreckers," worked year-round pulling bales of cotton, loads of lumber, and other valuable goods from the smashed hulls of ships that had run aground off Florida.

Clearly, something had to be done to warn ships away from Florida's dangerous shoals and headlands. The effort of marking the Florida Keys began in 1825, when a 65-foot brick lighthouse was erected at Key West. By the following year similar lighthouses stood on Garden Key, Sand Key, Cape Florida, and the Dry Tortugas, located about 70 miles west of Key West. (For a more complete account of the history of the Florida Keys lighthouses, see *Gulf Coast Lighthouses* by Bruce Roberts and Ray Jones [Globe Pequot, 1998]). In the decades that followed, lights also appeared at the mouth of the St. Johns River, Amelia Island, Cape Canaveral, and Jupiter Inlet. The Lighthouse Board hoped to define Florida "from end to end by a band of light." Although the board never achieved this ambitious goal, the new lighthouses made navigation safer and significantly reduced the number of wrecks.

Ironically, the Florida lighthouses were themselves only a little safer than the ships they guided along the coast. Even more exposed than their cousins to the north, these lighthouses were regularly battered by wind, rain, and high water. They lay under constant threat of gale and hurricane. A newly constructed brick tower erected just south of Daytona Beach in 1835 was overwhelmed so quickly that it never got a chance to display its light. Oil for the lamps had still not been delivered when a

A soaring brick light tower and a 46-foot tug help celebrate Florida's rich maritime history at the Ponce de Leon Inlet Lighthouse Museum.

powerful storm undermined its foundation, and the tower toppled over.

The sea and the wind were not the only dangers. War darkened the Florida coast on more than one occasion. One Florida lighthouse was even attacked by Native Americans.

BURNED BY INDIANS

By the mid-1830s the Seminoles had had their fill of the white man's broken promises, and war swept like a hurricane over the Florida peninsula. The isolated white settlements, which had sprung up since the arrival of the Americans in Florida, were open to attack. Especially vulnerable were the new lighthouses and their keepers.

On the afternoon of July 23, 1836, keeper John Thompson stepped from the dwelling-house kitchen of the Cape Florida Lighthouse on Biscayne Bay and was astonished to see a large war party of Native Americans running across a field toward him. Thompson shouted a warning to his assistant, an old black man named Henry, and the two rushed inside the brick-walled lighthouse. They had barely enough time to bar the door before the Native Americans piled up against it.

Thompson and Henry drove their attackers back with muskets. But the Native Americans answered with musket fire of their own, peppering the brick walls, splintering the door, and perforating a tin tank containing 225 gallons of lamp oil. Streams of oil squirted through the holes in the tank, soaking the floor and walls as well as the keeper and his helper. Flaming arrows set fire to the door, which, in turn, ignited the oil.

The defenders temporarily escaped the conflagration by scrambling up the wooden lighthouse steps. Once at the top, Thompson tried to cut away the steps so the Native Americans could not follow. But he gave up the effort when he saw that the flames were rapidly climbing after him, consuming the steps as they came. Thompson and Henry took refuge in the lantern, which was constructed mainly of iron, but the metal was already scorching hot. Both men realized, in horror, that they would soon be roasted alive.

"At last the awful moment arrived," Thompson wrote in his account of the attack. "The crackling flames burst around me. The savages at the same time began their hellish yells. [Henry] looked at me with tears in his eyes, but he could not speak."

Once more Thompson and Henry tried to escape the fire, this time by climbing out onto the narrow, metal platform surrounding the gallery. There they lay

The historic Cape Florida tower seen through the window of its dwelling.

flat on their bellies to avoid being shot by the Seminoles, who still had their muskets ready. "The lantern was now full of flame," said Thompson, "the lamps and glasses bursting and flying in all directions."

The iron beneath the men grew so hot that they could no longer bear the pain of touching it. Thompson had brought a musket and a keg of gunpowder with him to the lantern. He now jumped up and threw the powder keg down into the burning lighthouse. He meant to blow up the tower and put himself and his friend out of their misery, taking, he hoped, a few of the hated Seminoles along with him. With a tremendous roar the keg exploded, rocking the tower. But, said Thompson, "it had not the desired effect of blowing me into eternity." Instead, the explosion knocked out the flames.

By this time, Henry was already dead. He had tried to stand and was cut down by a Native American musket ball. And although the fire had died down, Thompson thought of jumping off the tower and joining his friend in death. "I was almost as bad off as before," he said, "a burning fever on me, my feet shot to pieces, no clothes to cover me, nothing to eat or drink, a hot sun overhead, a dead man by my side, no friend near or any to expect, and placed between seventy and eighty feet from the earth with no chance of getting down."

But friends were on the way. Sailors on the U.S. Navy schooner *Concord* had heard the explosion, and the warship soon appeared in the bay within sight of the ruined, but still-standing, lighthouse. A detachment of marines and seamen from the *Concord* landed at the light station a short time afterward and found that the Seminoles had retreated. They also discovered, much to their surprise, that the lighthouse keeper had survived the attack. There he was in the lantern waving at them and calling to them for help. But how to get him down from his high perch?

First the sailors tried to fly a line to Thompson with a kite. When this failed, they tied the line onto a ramrod and fired it up into the lantern with a musket. Employing the last of his strength, Thompson used the line to haul up a tail block, enabling two sailors to pull themselves up to the lantern. They, in turn, lowered Thompson to the ground. Treated for his burns and wounds in a military hospital, Thompson recovered and later continued his service as a lighthouse keeper. Thompson had lived through his worst experience in a Florida lighthouse. Not all Florida keepers would be so fortunate.

The glow of St. Augustine's massive first-order Fresnel lens warms this early morning scene. Damaged by a vandal's rifle shot in 1986, the big lens was repaired at a cost of $250,000.

AMELIA ISLAND LIGHT

Fernandina Beach, Florida — 1839

In 1820 the government had a 50-foot tower erected on Georgia's Cumberland Island. Its light marked the mouth of the St. Marys River, where it forms a natural border between Georgia and Florida. Following the annexation of Florida as a U.S. territory, the officials decided that the lighthouse would provide better service on the south bank of the river. So, in 1839, Cumberland Lighthouse was dismantled and moved to Amelia Island.

There it was reassembled on a piece of land the government had purchased from a local plantation owner. The height of the tower was raised by at least 14 feet as part of its reconstruction. Most of the additional height came in the form of a cylinder placed between the conical tower and the lantern section. When completed, the reconstructed lighthouse was 64 feet tall. It was equipped with a rotating optic with fourteen separate whale-oil lamps, each with its own reflector.

Named for the daughter of King George II of England, Amelia Island was once a swamp, infested not only with mosquitoes but also with pirates, smugglers, and slave traders. Slaves were brought to Amelia and then sold up the St. Marys River by a ring of smugglers known as the Moccasin Boys. These traffickers decoyed their slave-smuggling operations by spreading rumors of Native American attacks. Not surprisingly, they did not care to have other Florida settlers see what they were doing, since theirs was a particularly vile trade. The slaves were transported to Florida in small schooners; as many as 150 naked Africans might be packed into the dark holds of these ships, where many died of infection and exposure. It is said that in 1818 alone, as many as 1,000 slaves were brought to Amelia by the Moccasins and smuggled up the St. Marys.

Eventually, the slave smuggling diminished and was replaced by a vigorous trade in lumber, phosphate, shrimp, and military supplies. During the 1850s Florida's first railroad was laid in, connecting Amelia with Cedar Key on the far side of the state. All this activity brought more ships to the St. Marys and more people to Amelia.

Amelia Island Light is a classic Victorian structure, with a tapering whitewashed stone tower and a lantern room as a crown. But the keeper's two-story house, decked with galleries and canopies, reflects the antebellum flavor of the local architecture. Plenty of draped mosquito netting was a necessary feature of the house's interior decor.

The tower was given an unusual stairway made of granite shipped to Florida from the quarries in New England. Several times each night the keeper climbed the sixty-eight steps of the stairway in order to tend the mechanism that drove the rotating classical lens. The keeper rewound the device by raising heavy weights that dropped through the center of the tower. On more than one occasion, the cables holding the weights broke, causing them to snap back and chip the granite steps.

The Lighthouse Board had the Amelia Island tower renovated in 1885 and again in the early 1900s, raising the focal plane of the light to 105 feet above mean high water. The tower stands 2 miles from the north end of the island and 1 mile from the town of Fernandina.

Fitted with a third-order Fresnel lens, made by Barbier and Bernard of Paris, the light was originally powered by an oil lamp that burned with 1,500 candlepower. It, too, was rotated by a clockwork mechanism that had to be rewound every four hours.

Now electrified and automated, the light can be seen from 23 miles at sea. Sailors nearing shoals in Nassau Sound see a red flash, while others see a white flash. Amelia Island Light is still on active duty, guiding pleasure craft on the Intracoastal Waterway as well as tankers on the open Atlantic.

HOW TO GET THERE: *The lighthouse is located in a residential section of town on Lighthouse Circle but unfortunately is closed to the public. The only access is across private property posted* NO TRESPASSING, *but there is an excellent view from Atlantic Avenue. Call the Fernandina Beach Chamber of Commerce, (904) 261–3248, for more information.*

The Amelia Island Light was moved to its present site from Cumberland Island, Georgia, in 1839.

ST. JOHNS RIVER LIGHT

Mayport, Florida — 1830, 1835, AND 1859

A thoroughfare for warships, commercial freighters, fishing boats, and pleasure craft, Florida's St. Johns River is one of the busiest and most historic waterways in the country. The river has served as an inviting sanctuary for seafarers for more than 400 years. French explorer Jean Ribault established a small colony near the mouth of the river in 1565. Swept away by the tides of history, the French settlement was eventually supplanted by the Spanish, who built a mission here called San Juan del Puerto, or St. John of the Harbor. In time, the river became known as the San Juan. Later its name was anglicized and shortened to St. Johns.

A simple oil lamp hung on a pole may have been the first navigational light to guide ships into the St. Johns. The river's first official lighthouse was not completed until 1830, some fifteen years before Florida became a state. Among the earliest light towers built in what was then the territory of Florida, it cost more than $24,000 to build—a very large sum at the time—but lasted little more than five years. Surging tidal currents quickly undermined its foundation, and it was torn down in 1835.

That same year a second lighthouse was built on a site upriver from the original station, but by the early 1850s exasperated government officials realized the St. Johns River Lighthouse would have to be replaced yet again. This time the problem was sand rather than erosion. Dunes had piled up so high on the seaward side of the light that seamen could no longer see the beacon.

The river's third lighthouse was completed in 1858 and placed in operation on January 1 of the following year. Its 66-foot brick tower was fitted with a third-order Fresnel lens. The new beacon burned for little more than two years when the Civil War broke like a storm over the Southern coast. The St. Johns River Station fared better than most of the South's lighthouses, continuing to operate on and off until 1864. By then Union gunboats were using the light to guide them up the St. Johns, where they regularly ravaged Confederate positions. In order to blind the federal ships, the hard-pressed Southerners shot out the light.

Following the war the damage was repaired and the light relit. In 1887, brick masons added 15 feet to the tower, raising it to a height of 81 feet. The light served until 1929, when it was replaced by a lightship moored 7 miles from the mouth of the St. Johns.

HOW TO GET THERE: *Located on the Mayport Naval Air Station, the lighthouse is closed to the public. However, visitors are welcome to view the tower from nearby streets on the base. Visitors may enter the station during daylight hours after checking in at the security office. For information write to Public Affairs, Mayport Naval Air Station, Box 280032, Mayport, FL 32228–0032 or call (904) 270–5226.*

ST. JOHNS LIGHT

Mayport, Florida — 1954

Just south of Florida's St. Johns River stands one of the most unusual lighthouses in America. The typical U.S. light tower is cylinder shaped; made of stone, brick, or steel plate; and is usually more than a century old. But not this one. Built of concrete blocks, the St. Johns Lighthouse has an angular, modern appearance suggestive of the streamlined art deco structures popular during the mid-twentieth-century era. Perhaps not surprisingly, it is one of the more recently constructed U.S. lighthouses. It dates to 1954, the same year Elvis Presley released his first record, and so is only about as old as rock 'n' roll.

The 64-foot St. Johns tower has no lantern room. Instead, its flat roof supports a variety of antennas and other electronic gear and a revolving aeromarine optic producing approximately 200,000 candlepower. The white, flashing beacon can be seen from up to 22 miles out in the Atlantic and is used by ships moving along the Florida coast as well as naval vessels approaching their nearby base. The U.S. Navy base at Mayport is home to the supercarrier U.S.S. *Kennedy* and approximately thirty other warships. Planes and helicopters from the adjacent Naval Air Station regularly sweep over vast stretches of the Atlantic to keep watch for foreign submarines that might threaten the United States in time of war.

One night in 1942, not long after the United States had entered World War II, a German submarine surfaced just south of the point where the St. Johns Lighthouse now stands. Shielded by the dark, four German spies came ashore in a rubber raft and headed north by way of Jacksonville. Their immediate objective was to link up, after a few days, with a second group of Germans who had been dropped off on Long Island. Then the combined force was to sabotage key U.S. installations and industries. For reasons that have never been fully understood, the Long Island saboteurs voluntarily gave themselves up to a bewildered small-town policeman. This led to the arrest of the Florida group by the FBI. Eventually, six of the spies were executed and two others sentenced to long prison terms.

HOW TO GET THERE: *The St. Johns Light is located on the naval base at Mayport. The lighthouse is not open to the public, but it can be seen from a nearby naval-office compound. Visitors are allowed on the base during the day. You can get visitors' passes and directions to the lighthouse from the security office at the entrance to the base off State-A1A. Guided tours of ships are available on Saturday and Sunday. For more information contact Public Affairs, Naval Station, Mayport, FL 32228 or call (904) 270–5226.*

ST. AUGUSTINE LIGHT

St. Augustine, Florida — 1824 AND 1874

The Spanish may have built the first lighthouse in Florida, but no one knows for sure. Shortly after the U.S. acquisition of Florida in 1821, the government sent a team of inspectors to examine an old and somewhat mysterious tower near St. Augustine. The inspectors believed the Spanish may have used the three-story structure as a lighthouse. Built by early

Spanish settlers near the spot where Ponce de Leon had landed in 1513, the tower stood in a tiny, quarter-acre compound enclosed by walls 10 feet high and 16 inches thick. A small stone building inside the compound may have served as a home, perhaps for a lighthouse keeper.

St. Augustine was the leading port in the new U.S. territory of Florida, and Congress wanted a navigational light established there quickly. Taking for granted that the Spanish tower had, indeed, once served as a lighthouse, the officials ordered a lantern placed atop its third story as a temporary signal for mariners. Plans were made to refurbish the crumbling tower and outfit it with the latest navigational lamps and lens. But after an inspection of the building by St. Augustine customs collector John Rodman, officials decided against using the tower, which was only 44 feet tall, as a lighthouse. After a careful examination of the tower, with the help of a mason and a carpenter, Rodman declared the structure unsound and determined that the cost of renovation would soar to at least $5,000. In his report Rodman said he believed the building was a watchtower and had never been used as a lighthouse.

On orders from Washington, Rodman had a brick tower constructed a little less than 1,000 feet to the southwest of the Spanish compound. Completed in 1824, it rose 73 feet above sea level. Partly because it was provided with only a fourth-order lens, which was illuminated with oil lamps intensified by bowl-shaped reflectors, the usefulness of the light was limited to marking the entrance to the St. Augustine harbor.

Like most of the Florida lights, the St. Augustine Lighthouse came under assault by both man and nature. Early in the Civil War the Confederates darkened it. Then, shortly after it was relit in 1867, the tower was threatened by the sea, as storm-driven erosion brought tides to within just 48 feet of its foundation. Consequently, the Lighthouse Board decided to build a new tower on a more secure location about a half mile away on Anastasia Island.

Construction began in 1872, but funds ran out

The black-and-white striped St. Augustine tower and its brick keeper's dwelling both date to the 1870s.

In the past, only birds and lighthouse keepers could enjoy this view of old St. Augustine.

before the brickwork could be carried up more than a few feet. Meanwhile, the sea rapidly closed in on the old lighthouse; water lapped within 10 feet at high tide. Hoping to slow the erosion, workers hurriedly laid down a jetty of brush and coquina, a soft limestone composed of shells and coral, and this stopgap measure bought valuable time.

The interruption in funding proved only temporary, and with money flowing again, workers were able to complete the new lighthouse in less than two years; the keeper lit its first-order lens on October 15, 1874. Meanwhile, the sea continued its advance on the old tower, finally enveloping it in 1880.

The new light was more powerful than the old one had been; it had a focal plane 161 feet above the sea and could be seen for 19 miles. Painted with barberpole stripes to make it easier to identify during the day, the tower was a near duplicate of others built in the 1870s at Cape Hatteras, Bodie Island, and Currituck Beach.

HOW TO GET THERE: *This is one of the few lighthouses in a populated area. From downtown St. Augustine, take the bridge toward St. Augustine Beach. Turn across the Alligator Farm to 81 Lighthouse Avenue; the lighthouse, with its white and black spiral stripes, is on the left side of the highway.*

The Junior League of St. Augustine has restored the keeper's house and opened it as a lighthouse museum. Exhibits in the house tell of the social life of this historic city and of the many famous people who visited the lighthouse. Beautiful live oak trees surround the complex and border the sweeping front yard of the house. It is perhaps the most elegant keeper's quarters in the South, and the restoration and exhibits are among the best in the South.

The tower is open to the public. For more information contact St. Augustine Lighthouse, Inc., at 81 Lighthouse Avenue, St. Augustine, FL 32084; (904) 829–0745.

PONCE DE LEON INLET LIGHT

Ponce Inlet, Florida — 1887

The first lighthouse built for Ponce de Leon Inlet, then called Mosquito Inlet, collapsed before its lamps had ever been lit. Oil for the lamps still had not been delivered in 1835 when a storm undermined the tower's foundation. Hostile Seminoles prevented work-

men from rescuing the tower from further damage, and it soon toppled over and was left in ruins.

Nearly fifty years later a new lighthouse was erected, this time on the north side of what is now known as Ponce de Leon Inlet. Built with brick

Preparing to raise Old Glory at the Ponce de Leon Inlet Lighthouse.

This view, suggestive of a conch shell, awaits visitors at the top of the spiral staircase at the Ponce de Leon Inlet Lighthouse.

shipped south from Baltimore, the tower is 168 feet tall, making it the second tallest lighthouse on the East Coast. Bringing materials ashore for the construction of the tower was dangerous work, and at least one man was killed in the effort: Maj. O. E. Babcock, engineer of the Fifth and Sixth Lighthouse Districts.

Lit in the autumn of 1887, the Ponce de Leon Light helped fill the 95-mile gap between the St. Augustine and Cape Canaveral lights. The redbrick conical tower displayed a flashing white light that could be seen from 19 miles at sea. Drapes were drawn around the tower's third-order Fresnel lens during the day to prevent the sun from cracking its prisms or concentrating sunlight and starting fires in the lantern room. Oil for the remote lighthouse was lightered in small boats and carried by hand to the lantern room, 203 spiraling steps from the ground. Kerosene later replaced oil as a fuel.

This lighthouse served all sorts of traffic, including Bahama-bound, Prohibition-era rumrunners, who often pulled into the inlet at night to avoid trouble on the reefs. It was taken out of service in 1970, however, because the beacon atop the New Smyrna Coast Guard Station made it redundant. The tower stood dormant and vulnerable for two years until it was deeded to the townspeople of Ponce Inlet in 1972. Then, in 1983, the old light was reinstated when a sprouting condo-

minium development at New Smyrna Beach obscured the nearby Coast Guard Station's beacon.

HOW TO GET THERE: *Take State A1A south from Daytona Beach (the Atlantic Ocean will be on the left-hand side of the road). At Port Orange, go straight on the paved unnumbered road that continues south through Wilbur-by-the-Sea to Ponce Inlet (the* NO OUTLET *signs mean you are on the correct road). The tall brick lighthouse will be straight ahead when you near the inlet.*

The Ponce de Leon Inlet Lighthouse Preservation Association, Inc., a nonprofit organization, has restored and opened a complex of buildings at the lighthouse site. The tower is open and can be climbed. Several of the keeper's houses display lighthouse exhibits, and as a group they form one of the best lighthouse museums on the entire East Coast. In the lens exhibit building, be sure to see the display of the magnificent, first-order Cape Canaveral lens and the third-order Fresnel lens from the Ponce de Leon Inlet Light.

The complex is open during daylight hours; there is a small admission fee. For additional information contact Ponce de Leon Inlet Lighthouse Museum, 4931 South Peninsula Drive, Ponce Inlet, FL 32127; (904) 761–1821.

CAPE CANAVERAL LIGHT

Cape Canaveral Air Force Station, Florida — 1848 AND 1868

Sometimes construction of a lighthouse did more harm than good to shipping. In 1848 the government built a lighthouse to warn ships away from a bank of dangerous shoals extending several miles to the east of Florida's Cape Canaveral. But the brick tower was only 65 feet tall, and its light was so weak that mariners were already over the shoals before they could see it. Some ships ran aground on the shoals when their captains brought them too close to shore while searching the landward horizon for the Canaveral Light.

In 1859 the Lighthouse Board tried to correct the situation by raising a second, much taller tower at Canaveral. But construction crews had just started on the foundation when the Civil War put a stop to their efforts. At war's end they went back to work, and the new tower was completed by the summer of 1868. A cast-iron cylinder lined with brick, the tower stood 139 feet above sea level, and its light could be seen from 18 miles at sea, a distance more than sufficient to keep ships away from the Canaveral shoals.

Like many lighthouses built on the shifting sands of the South's Atlantic coast, this second Canaveral tower was eventually threatened by erosion. Engineers fought back against the encroaching ocean with stone jetties, but the tides kept gaining on the lighthouse. In 1893, with waves crashing within 200 feet of the tower foundation, the board had the structure dismantled and rebuilt more than a mile west of its original location.

Since 1964 the Canaveral Light has been known as Cape Kennedy Lighthouse; the name change honors the fallen U.S. president who committed the country to placing a man on the moon before 1970. Sailors still use the old light to navigate safely around the Canaveral shoals, but for decades now they have often seen other bright lights on the cape—rockets rushing skyward from the nearby Kennedy Space Center.

HOW TO GET THERE: *Still an operating lighthouse, this nineteenth-century navigation marker has flashed its beam across the bows of modern vessels with names such as Mercury, Atlas, Gemini, Titan, and Apollo. The Air Force Station is accessible to the public only by bus tours from Kennedy Space Center. From I–95 or US 1, take the NASA Parkway; turn northeast onto County 3, and follow the signs to the Kennedy Space Center. Not all tours pass by the lighthouse. For more information on tour routes and costs, contact Spaceport USASM, Visitors Center TWS, Kennedy Space Center, FL 32899; (321) 452–2121.*

An Atlas Centaur 9 takes off at Cape Canaveral, within sight of the Cape Canaveral Light. (Courtesy NASA)

JUPITER INLET LIGHT

Jupiter, Florida — 1860

A terrible hurricane ripped through Jupiter Inlet in 1928, knocking out the lighthouse's newly installed electrical system. When the station's emergency generator failed to start, the shoreline fell dark just at the time when passing ships most needed guidance. Keeper Charles Seabrook, despite a severely infected hand, reinstalled the light's old mineral lamps but was too weakened by pain to operate them manually. Seabrook's sixteen-year-old son persuaded his father to let him climb the tower, by now an inverted pendulum swaying 17 inches off-center. The boy proved himself a man as he turned the light by hand and kept it moving for four harrowing hours.

Trouble shrouded the Jupiter Light from the beginning. Angry Seminoles, heat, shallow water, and mosquitoes delayed its lighting for nearly four years after construction started in the late 1850s. Since the inlet was too shallow for navigation at that time, building materials were unloaded from large sailing vessels at Indian River Inlet and lightered the 35 miles to Jupiter Inlet in shallow-draft scows. To move the 500 tons of material needed to build the lighthouse, the grueling trek had to be repeated fifty times. The light was finally fired up in July 1860.

The light burned for little more than a year before it was extinguished by Confederate raiders who hoped to impede the movement of blockading Union ships. The men in gray removed and hid the big Fresnel lens. At the end of the Civil War, Capt. James A. Armour, who was to enjoy a record forty-year career as keeper of Jupiter Inlet Light, found the lens buried in Jupiter Creek. He had it reinstalled and working by the end of 1866.

At Jupiter Inlet, Armour lived a life even more

The bright red Jupiter Inlet tower stands in sharp contrast to its surroundings.

Congress authorized construction of Jupiter Inlet Lighthouse because of the treacherous geology surrounding Jupiter Island, where the Loxahatchee River meets the Atlantic Ocean. A large reef located just offshore is a formidable obstacle to westbound ships needing to cross the Gulf Stream before heading north. The first-order lens, with its focal plane 146 feet above the sea, serves a dual function, warning vessels of the reef and guiding ships along the coast.

George Gordon Meade designed the tower, with its iron latticework frame for the lantern windows and portholes over the lantern gallery. Meade, though best known for defeating Gen. Robert E. Lee in the Battle of Gettysburg, built many of Florida's lighthouses, including the revolutionary screw-pile lights of the Florida Reef.

The Jupiter Inlet Lighthouse has been placed on the National Register of Historic Places. Indeed, it is among the most storied and historic of American lights. The tower itself was built on a prehistoric Native American mound of oyster shells. The route of the Indian River steamer ended at Jupiter, and Florida's famed "Celestial Railroad" began at Jupiter and ran through Mars, Venus, and Juno. A famed lifesaving station was set up at the inlet in 1885 to deal with shipwrecks. A telegraph station was built on the grounds of the lighthouse in 1911. Nearby the lighthouse was a schoolhouse built for the children of Florida's early-nineteenth-century pioneers. Many schoolmarms married lighthouse keepers, who were among the few available bachelors. Descendants of these unions still live in the area.

Storms continue to plague the Jupiter coast. In 1872 a powerful gale rolled out of the northeast, driving the steamer *Victor* aground just south of the Jupiter Inlet. The passengers and crew aboard the freighter might never have reached shore without the assistance of the Jupiter Lighthouse keeper. No one was killed, but three dogs were apparently orphaned by the accident. The keeper adopted the dogs, naming them Vic, Storm, and Wreck.

HOW TO GET THERE: *This lighthouse, painted a bright red, can be seen from the US 1 bridge over Jupiter Inlet at Jupiter, north of West Palm Beach. Call the lighthouse at (561) 747–8380 for tour information.*

His coloring a bit more subtle than that of the lighthouse behind him, a grumpy looking pelican poses at Jupiter Inlet.

isolated than that of most other lighthouse keepers. When he brought his new bride to the inlet in 1867, she was the only white woman for 100 miles.

Although a sign in front of the lighthouse says, IT HAS NOT MISSED A NIGHT IN OVER 100 YEARS, the light was, in fact, darkened briefly in the 1950s when a hurricane knocked out the windows in the lantern and smashed the irreplaceable bull's-eye lens. This misfortune might have doomed the light had not technician James Maher painstakingly cemented the shards back into their original configuration and bound them together with a brass framework.

HILLSBORO INLET LIGHT

Hillsboro Inlet, Florida — 1907

The Hillsboro Inlet Lighthouse was not built in Florida but rather in the Midwest. Constructed by a Chicago company at a cost of $90,000, it was shipped down the Mississippi to St. Louis, where it delighted crowds at the 1904 Exposition. When the Exposition closed, the lighthouse seemed very out of place. Eventually, it was purchased by the government and moved to Hillsboro Inlet, where it began service as a navigational light in 1907. The last beach lighthouse erected in Florida, it marks the northern approaches to Miami.

The lighthouse was anchored by six huge iron piles, a design innovation intended to ease the strain of wind and water on the structure. The lower third of the octagonal pyramid skeleton was painted white and the upper two-thirds painted black, distinguishing it from its redbrick counterparts at Jupiter Inlet and Cape Florida.

At first the light was fueled by kerosene, which had to be carried by keepers up the 175 steps in the central stair cylinder to the lantern room, 136 feet above mean sea level. The lens rotated on a mercury-filled reservoir and was driven by a clockwork mechanism powered by a weight. The keeper had to raise the weight by hand every half hour.

The light was converted to electric power in the late

The Hillsboro Inlet Lighthouse was displayed at the 1904 Exposition in St. Louis.

1920s and in 1966 was upgraded to two million candlepower. The lens makes one complete revolution every forty seconds, with one-second flashes every twenty seconds. Its light can be seen from 25 miles away.

During the light's early years, a series of unexplained fires broke out in the area near the tower. After much investigation, it was discovered that the fires had been ignited by sunlight concentrated by the powerful lens. To solve this problem, a shield was constructed on the landward side.

A plaque near the lighthouse commemorates the death of James E. Hamilton, the legendary mailman who walked barefoot on his delivery route from Jupiter Light to Miami. Hamilton drowned in 1887 while trying to bring mail across Hillsboro Inlet.

Hillsboro Inlet, named for the Earl of Hillsboro, who surveyed much of Florida during the 1700s, has been a target for many severe storms and hurricanes. But the lighthouse, with its sturdy pile legs, has stood firm.

HOW TO GET THERE: *This lighthouse is located on State A1A between Pompano Beach and Boca Raton. Still in operation and maintained by the Coast Guard, it is not open to the public, but the tower can be viewed from the State A1A bridge over the inlet. An even better view can be had from the beach on the south side of the inlet.*

Statue of James E. Hamilton, the barefoot mailman who walked his delivery route from Jupiter Light to Miami. Hamilton drowned while bringing mail across Hillsboro Inlet.

CAPE FLORIDA LIGHT

Key Biscayne, Florida — CA. 1825

Not long after the construction of the Key West Light, a 65-foot lighthouse tower was erected at the opposite (northeastern) end of the island chain. Built in 1825 on Cape Florida, some 30 miles north of Carysfort Reef at the northern entrance to Biscayne Bay, the brick tower had walls 5 feet thick.

Severely damaged during the 1836 Seminole siege, the lighthouse remained out of service for nearly ten years, largely because the Native Americans made the site too dangerous for repair crews. When reconstruction was finally under way in 1846, workers discovered that the lighthouse had been the victim not only of Native Americans but also of fraud. Samuel B. Lincoln, the contractor who had built the tower more than twenty years earlier, had given it hollow walls, saving himself nearly 50 percent on the cost of brick.

The reef-laden coast of southeastern Florida had been claiming ships since the area was discovered in 1497 by John Cabot. And in the 1800s, even with its light burning again, Cape Florida remained deadly. Ship captains complained that, all too often, they could not see the light. So, following a series of disastrous wrecks during the early 1850s, the board raised the tower to 100 feet above sea level, fitting it with a new Fresnel lens.

Relations with the Seminoles were not always hostile. The Native Americans regularly traded with the keepers and their families; in fact, they occasionally took the hospitality of the keepers a bit too far. One evening a Seminole came to the lighthouse keeper to barter. Finding everyone in bed, he slipped into bed himself with one of the children, where, to the horror of the keeper's wife, he was found the next morning.

During the Civil War the lighthouse had a new set of enemies, the Confederates, who destroyed the illuminating apparatus in 1861. Restored in 1866, it remained in service another

twelve years, after which it was replaced by a new lighthouse at Fowey Rocks, 2 miles southeast of Key Biscayne. But the story of the Cape Florida Lighthouse did not end there. During the 1970s the Coast Guard decided to refurbish and recommission it. Coincidentally, the old sentinel was relighted in 1978, exactly one hundred years after it had been extinguished.

Palms frame the soaring Cape Florida tower on Key Biscayne, shown here as it looked before its recent restoration.

The photo above, taken before the restoration, shows how wind and weather had clawed the bricks of the Cape Florida tower.

Now a popular attraction, the tower has been completely refurbished and painted white. (Courtesy Bob and Sandra Shanklin)

HOW TO GET THERE: *Located only a few miles from downtown Miami, this lighthouse is in a tropical setting of coconut palms and Australian pines at the Bill Baggs State Recreation Area. It can be reached by taking the Rickenbacker Causeway from the southern terminus of I–95. After the causeway, follow Crandon Boulevard to the lighthouse; avoid taking the interstate during the rush hour, when traffic moves at a snail's pace. There is a toll fee to get onto the island and an admission charge to the Bill Baggs State Recreation Area.*

Once inside the recreation area, it seems impossible that a major city is nearby; thick woods lead down to a white-sand beach. The lighthouse is located near the beach. It has been handsomely renovated and is now one of the most attractive light towers in America. Take your camera. For additional information contact the Cape Florida Light, Bill Baggs State Recreation Area, 1200 South Crandon Boulevard, Key Biscayne, Florida 33149; (305) 361–5811.

FOWEY ROCKS LIGHT

Off Key Biscayne, Florida — 1878

No Native Americans would likely have attacked the Fowey Rocks Light Station—as they did the one on Cape Florida—since it stood in the open ocean nearly 10 miles from shore and out of sight from the mainland. Established in 1878 to replace the Cape Florida Light and to mark a troublesome shoal, this was one of the most remote and exposed lighthouses ever built.

The Fowey Rocks shoal took its name from the HMS *Fowey,* a British Navy frigate that ran aground here in 1748 with tragic results. The ship was lost along with most of her crew. Over the years many other hapless vessels followed the *Fowey* to their doom on this murderous reef.

Aware that the Cape Florida Light failed to give adequate warning of the shoal, the Lighthouse Board decided to place a light station directly over Fowey Rocks. It was not a decision the board took lightly, as the lighthouse would have to be built over open water in a region frequented by raging gales and killer hurricanes. Since making daily journeys back and forth to the mainland was too dangerous and time-consuming, workers had to live at the construction site on a hastily erected platform. Storms often blew in unexpectedly, throwing up such high waves that they almost carried away the entire construction crew. On several different occasions ships almost smashed into the unfinished lighthouse. Two of these ran aground on the rocks, making the need for a light all the more obvious.

When completed, the Fowey Rocks tower stood 100 feet tall, its spidery iron legs firmly anchored to the hard, subsurface coral reef. The tower was built on eight pilings, driven not just into the coral, but through massive iron discs resting on a stabilized concrete foundation. This arrangement has proven so durable that the tower has survived for more than 120 years, during which time dozens of ferocious hurricanes and countless gales have swept over Fowey Rocks. The tower's skeleton structure exposes a minimum of surface to destructive winds.

Keepers reached the lantern room by way of a spiral staircase inside the central, steel cylinder. There a first-order Fresnel lens flashed out an alternating white and red warning beacon. Before it was installed at the Fowey Rocks Station, the big Fresnel had fascinated crowds at the Lighthouse Service exhibit in the 1876 Philadelphia Centennial Exposition. The huge lens served until the station was automated in 1974, and it was replaced by a high-powered aeromarine optic. The light flashes white or red every ten seconds and can be seen from about 15 miles away.

HOW TO GET THERE: *Fowey Rocks Light Station is now part of Key Biscayne National Park. For more information on the park and boating in the vicinity of the lighthouse, call (305) 230–7275.*

Like an illustration from a Jules Verne novel, the Fowey Rocks Lighthouse reflects the creative imagination—and engineering skill—of an earlier day. (Courtesy Bob and Sandra Shanklin)

The bull's-eyes of this huge first-order Fresnel, now on display at Ponce Inlet, once focused the powerful flashes of the Cape Canaveral Lighthouse.

CHAPTER FIVE

FRESNELS:

Chandeliers That Save Lives

The business end of a lighthouse is, of course, at the top. The lighting apparatus is kept in the lantern room as high above sea level as the tower and the elevation of the site can make possible. Height adds to the beacon's range, or distance from which it can be seen.

But equally important to the beacon's effectiveness is the strength of the light itself. Usually a lens, mirror, or other optical device is used to concentrate the light, often into a single brilliant flash. For many years, the most efficient way of doing this was with a Fresnel lens.

Invented in 1822 by French physicist Augustin Fresnel, these big prismatic glass lenses were designed to snatch every flicker of light from even the smallest lamp and concentrate it into a powerful beam that could be seen from dozens of miles away. Fresnel's elegant lenses did their job so well that they soon became standard equipment in lighthouses throughout much of the world.

However, the new Fresnel technology was virtually ignored for several decades in the United States, where Winslow Lewis's far less effective parabolic reflectors were employed right up until the middle of the nineteenth century. One reason the United States was slow to adopt the Fresnel system was the considerable expense of the highly polished lenses, which had to be imported from France. Another was the bureaucratic fussiness of Stephen Pleasonton, the U.S. Treasury auditor who served for many years as head of the so-called lighthouse establishment. Displaying undisguised favoritism for Lewis, a personal friend, Pleasonton continued to equip U.S. lighthouses with his outdated reflectors, even though they were demonstrably inferior to Fresnel lenses. Following the release of a highly critical report written by Lewis's own nephew, Pleasonton was forced into retirement.

In 1852, stewardship of America's navigational lights passed to a Lighthouse Board consisting of military officers, engineers, harbor masters, and experienced seamen. The board immediately undertook a complete overhaul of America's ill-equipped and, in many cases, sadly neglected lighthouses. As part of this effort, most lighthouses were fitted with sparkling new Fresnel lenses. Some of these lenses, installed during the years before the Civil War, remain in service to this day.

Remarkably, Fresnel lenses are as effective and useful today as they were 150 years ago. This is a claim that can be made for very few devices. The fact is, few significant improvements have been

Fresnel lenses were artistic, though highly practical, creations of eighteenth-century technology. This revolving first-order lens emitted bright flashes seen from up to 25 miles away.

The Fresnel concept proved so effective that it far outlived the old-fashioned whale oil and kerosene lamps that once lit the lenses. Nowadays, electricity does the job. Notice the spare bulb.

made in the design of prismatic lenses since the days of Augustin Fresnel. Unlike so many other technologies—transportation, for instance—this one reached its peak of sophistication very early in the industrial revolution. Long before the development of space rockets, jet airliners, automobiles, or even of large steam locomotives, Fresnel lenses were already shining in lighthouse towers. To fully appreciate the contrast, consider that some early Fresnels were delivered in horse-drawn carts to the light stations where they were to serve.

Although a Fresnel lens looks like a single piece of molded glass, it is not. The lens consists of individual prisms—sometimes more than a thousand of them—fitted into a metal frame. This makes them look like giant glass beehives. It also makes them rather delicate.

Fresnels come in a variety of sizes, referred to as "orders." The huge first-order lenses, such as the one that once served at the Cape Canaveral Lighthouse (now on display at the Ponce Inlet, Florida, Museum) are 6 feet or more in diameter and up to 12 feet tall. The smallest lenses, designated sixth-order, are only about 1 foot in diameter.

The larger and more powerful first-, second-, and third-order lenses were intended for use in coastal lighthouses. The smaller fourth-, fifth-, and sixth-order lenses saw use mostly in harbor and river lighthouses. Specially designed 3.5-order lenses—a compromise between the larger and smaller sizes—were frequently used to guide vessels on the Great Lakes.

While Fresnel lenses are as effective and powerful as any so-called modern optical device, they require considerable care and must be cleaned and polished frequently by hand. The larger Fresnels are quite heavy, sometimes weighing in at more than a ton. As a consequence, the mechanisms that turn flashing Fresnel lenses must be large and are cumbersome. Despite their size, the old lenses are quite delicate, easily damaged, and almost impossible to repair. For all of these reasons, the efficiency-

Some Fresnel lenses are enormous. This shot was taken from inside the first-order lens at St. Augustine, which is more than six feet wide.

minded Coast Guard has replaced many Fresnels with plastic lenses or airport-type beacons that are lighter in weight and easier to maintain. Many of the old lenses have ended up in museums where the public can enjoy them. However, some Fresnels have been sold off to private collectors by antiques dealers.

Existing Fresnel lenses are practically irreplaceable. When they are destroyed by storms or vandalism, as unfortunately sometimes happens, the Coast Guard must replace them with a modern optic or a Fresnel previously removed from another lighthouse. The cost of manufacturing new Fresnel lenses is prohibitively high, possibly running into the millions of dollars.

During the nineteenth century, Fresnel lenses were hand ground and hand polished by the poorest classes of French laborers, including children, who often worked for pennies a day. It is ironic that the handiwork of these unremembered workers can be counted among the most practical, durable, and handsome devices ever made. No one will ever know how many lives have been saved by these fine old lenses or how many accidents were avoided because their guiding light could be seen on the horizon.

The first-order lens at St. Augustine is rotated by heavy, factory-style machinery.

FOR FURTHER INFORMATION ON LIGHTHOUSES

Lighthouse Digest
P.O. Box 1690
Wells, ME 04090
(207) 646–0515
www.lighthousedigest.com

U.S. Lighthouse Society
244 Kearney Street, Fifth Floor
San Francisco, CA 94108
www.lanternroom.com

U.S. Coast Guard
Historian's Office
2100 Second Street SW
Washington, DC 20593

American Lighthouse Foundation
P.O. Box 889
Wells, ME 04090
(207) 646–0515
www.lighthousefoundation.org

Outer Banks Lighthouse Society
P.O. Box 1005
Morehead City, NC 28557
www.outer-banks.com/lighthouse-society

Florida Lighthouse Association
P.O. Box 340028
Tampa, FL 33694
www.floridalighthouses.org

LIGHTHOUSES INDEX

Numerals in italics indicate photograph only.

ABOUT THE AUTHORS

BRUCE ROBERTS and his wife, Cheryl, who helped with the research for this book, live on North Carolina's Outer Banks, not far from the Cape Lookout Lighthouse. For many years Bruce was Senior Travel Photographer for *Southern Living* magazine. He started his career working as a photographer for newspapers in Tampa, Florida, and Charlotte, North Carolina. He is the recipient of many photography awards, and some of his photos are in the permanent collection of the Smithsonian Institution.

RAY JONES is a freelance writer and publishing consultant living in Monterey, California. He began his writing career working as a reporter for weekly newspapers in Texas. He has served as an editor for Time-Life Books, as founding editor of *Albuquerque Living* magazine, as a senior editor and writing coach at *Southern Living* magazine, and as founder and publisher of Country Roads Press. Ray grew up in Macon, Georgia, where he was inspired by the writing of Ernest Hemingway and William Faulkner, and worked his way through college as a disc jockey.

The Ponce de Leon Inlet Lighthouse on the Atlantic coast of Florida stands on this massive brick base. A staircase of more than 200 steps spirals inside the 175-foot tower.